Editor-in-Chief and Founder:
  Lyndon H. LaRouche, Jr.
Editorial Board: *Lyndon H. LaRouche, Jr. , Helga
  Zepp-LaRouche, Robert Ingraham, Tony
  Papert, Gerald Rose, Dennis Small, Jeffrey
  Steinberg, William Wertz*
Co-Editors: *Robert Ingraham, Tony Papert*
Technology: *Marsha Freeman*
Books: *Katherine Notley*
Ebooks: *Richard Burden*
Graphics: *Alan Yue*
Photos: *Stuart Lewis*
Circulation Manager: *Stanley Ezrol*

INTELLIGENCE DIRECTORS
Counterintelligence: *Jeffrey Steinberg, Michele
  Steinberg*
Economics: *John Hoefle, Marcia Merry Baker,
  Paul Gallagher*
History: *Anton Chaitkin*
Ibero-America: *Dennis Small*
Russia and Eastern Europe: *Rachel Douglas*
United States: *Debra Freeman*

INTERNATIONAL BUREAUS
Bogotá: *Miriam Redondo*
Berlin: *Rainer Apel*
Copenhagen: *Tom Gillesberg*
Houston: *Harley Schlanger*
Lima: *Sara Madueño*
Melbourne: *Robert Barwick*
Mexico City: *Gerardo Castilleja Chávez*
New Delhi: *Ramtanu Maitra*
Paris: *Christine Bierre*
Stockholm: *Ulf Sandmark*
United Nations, N.Y.C.: *Leni Rubinstein*
Washington, D.C.: *William Jones*
Wiesbaden: *Göran Haglund*

ON THE WEB
e-mail: eirns@larouchepub.com
www.larouchepub.com
www.executiveintelligencereview.com
www.larouchepub.com/eiw
Webmaster: *John Sigerson*
Assistant Webmaster: *George Hollis*
Editor, Arabic-language edition: *Hussein Askary*

EIR (ISSN 0273-6314) *is published weekly
(50 issues), by EIR News Service, Inc.,
P.O. Box 17390, Washington, D.C. 20041-0390.
(703) 297-8434*

European Headquarters: *E.I.R. GmbH, Postfach
Bahnstrasse 9a, D-65205, Wiesbaden, Germany*
Tel: 49-611-73650
Homepage: http://www.eir.de
e-mail: info@eir.de
Director: Georg Neudecker

Montreal, Canada: 514-461-1557
eir@eircanada.ca

Denmark: EIR - Danmark, Sankt Knuds Vej 11,
basement left, DK-1903 Frederiksberg, Denmark.
Tel.: +45 35 43 60 40, Fax: +45 35 43 87 57. e-mail:
eirdk@hotmail.com.

Mexico City: EIR, Sor Juana Inés de la Cruz 242-2
Col. Agricultura C.P. 11360
Delegación M. Hidalgo, México D.F.
Tel. (5525) 5318-2301
eirmexico@gmail.com

Better Ideas
Are Taking Over

EIR Contents

www.larouchepub.com   Volume 45, Number 14, April 6, 2018

Left to right: Russian President Vladimir Putin, Chinese President Xi Jinping, and U.S. President Donald Trump.

Cover This Week

BETTER IDEAS ARE TAKING OVER

I. The Wreck of the Anglo-Dutch System

II. LaRouche's Ideas on the World Stage

III. U.S. Idea More Mature than Europe

The Fraud of 'Western Democracy': Who are the Real Authoritarians?

by Robert Ingraham

March 31—During the last fifteen consecutive months we have witnessed an ongoing, continual, escalating effort on the part of the British establishment and its friends in the United States to prevent President Donald Trump from pursuing a path of normalizing relations with Russia and China—to find means, despite the difficulties and disagreements, to move the world away from super-power confrontation and to explore avenues of peaceful cooperation.

The entirety of the so-called "Russiagate" affair and all of the hoopla surrounding Special Counsel Robert Mueller's efforts to "pin something" on Donald Trump must be correctly viewed within this framework, and not simplistically—and incorrectly—as a product of "partisan politics." Similarly, the latest unhinged efforts by the unstable Theresa May to use the alleged poisoning of Sergei Skripal to agitate for an escalated crusade against Russia, fall within the same oligarchical playbook.

At the time of Donald Trump's election to the Presidency, Lyndon LaRouche insisted that Trump's unexpected victory must be understood as part of a growing international revolt against the policies of the trans-Atlantic power structure, not simply as a result of a domestic U.S. political phenomenon.

As we have seen in the results of the recent Italian elections—as well as in the receptivity of many European nations to China's Belt and Road Initiative—this revolt against the financial, economic and foreign policies of the European Union and the Anglo-Ameri-can establishment is continuing to spread and is gaining momentum. Circles around the British Crown are now so desperate that the British Prime Minister herself has taken the public lead in this latest anti-Russia screed. The fact that the charges now being leveled against Russia are such transparent falsehoods that many nations are refusing to go along with them, is a clear indication of just how desperate the British are. All of their post-1989 plans for a global New World Order of trans-Atlantic hegemony are crumbling.

The New Clash of Civilizations

As the pressures against Donald Trump mount, all stops are being pulled out in trans-Atlantic establishment media to inundate the populations of Europe and the United States with a political analysis which goes something like this:

"We are now facing a period of crisis, the worst

FBI

The hitmen and assassins of the Anglo-Dutch Liberal order. Left to right, James Comey, Barack Obama, and Robert Mueller.

The fabrication of a fake threat to the United States.

since the end of the cold war and perhaps even the most dangerous since the end of World War II. The world is now dividing between 'free' and 'non-free' states. On the one side are the 'Western Democracies,'—sometimes called 'liberal democracies'—those nations committed to human rights, liberal economics, and personal freedom. These nations—particularly Great Britain and the United States—bear a responsibility to defend 'freedom and democracy.' Opposed are the growing forces of totalitarianism—closed nations that are aggressive, anti-democratic, and corrupt, and which routinely restrict freedom and violate human rights. These nations are now challenging the benevolent post-World War II hegemony of the Western Democracies, and for the sake of all humanity they must be opposed."

Empiricists and nominalists like to gives names to things, because with a name, a whole gestalt of emotions, prejudices and subsumed predicates can be summoned forth by the mere mention of a particular name or phrase—emotional prejudices which are "built into" the name—thus predisposing the reader or listener to think in a certain way whenever the name is mentioned. The name that has been attached to this fabricated totalitarian threat is the "New Authoritarianism."

The New Authoritarianism is now being discussed everywhere. In establishment media as divergent as *Foreign Policy*, *Foreign Affairs*, the *Economist*, the *Financial Times*, the website of Chatham House (the Royal Institute for International Affairs), the *Atlantic*, Freedom House, the *Weekly Standard*, the *American Spectator*, *The New Yorker*—and many more—major pieces have been published warning of the new totalitarian threat. Usually, the term used is the New Authoritarianism, sometimes it is Modern Authoritarianism, and in regard to China's Belt and Road Initiative, a new epithet has been created called Market Authoritarianism.

Many world leaders are named in such articles as authoritarian and/or totalitarian, including Kim Jong-un of North Korea, Bashar al-Assad of Syria, and Recep Tayyip Erdogan of Turkey. However, the bulk of attention in all of these writings is given over to discussion of Vladimir Putin and Xi Jinping. They are the primary targets. They are the aggressive totalitarian threats to the West. One of the most insane examples of the propaganda now being spewed out is an article which appeared March 14 in the London *Telegraph*. Written by Allister Heath—the editor of the *Sunday Telegraph*—the article, "We need a new world alliance to take on totalitarian capitalists in Russia and China," says the following:

> We must take the lead in building a new global military and economic alliance of like-minded countries committed to the promotion of capitalism and liberal democracy. NATO is no

longer enough.… The new network should be based on mutual self-interest and respectful of national sovereignty; it would be open to all liberal democracies that practice capitalism, and that respect human rights, intellectual property and privacy. It should be a values alliance, governed by a treaty guaranteeing military self-help and seeking the freest possible trade in goods and services. America would be a member, as would Canada, India, Israel, Australia, Japan, New Zealand, France … and many others. Such an alliance would be the biggest shift in geopolitics since the creation of the UN. It would dramatically shift the global balance of power, and allow the liberal democracies finally to fight back. It would endow the world with the sorts of robust institutions that are required to contain Russia and China.…

In the years following the break-up of the Soviet Union, a proposal was advanced that the world was now entering a new era, one in which the geopolitical rivalry of the Cold War would be replaced by a "Clash of Civilizations." This term was first used in 1990 by the British-American operative Bernard Lewis. It was then popularized by Samuel Huntington in an article in *Foreign Affairs* magazine in 1992, and then again in his 1996 book, *The Clash of Civilizations*. Many people who have heard the term believe it refers to the alleged threat posed to world by radical Islam, and certainly Hun-

The British empire's daily newspaper, the Telegraph, *heightens offensive against the U.S., Russia, China alliance.*

tington's thesis, and the way it was elaborated by others, was used to justify the western invasions of Iraq and Afghanistan. However, the primary argument of Huntington's work was not about Islam at all.

He begins by defining the core values of the Western World, which he identifies with human rights, liberal democracy, and the capitalist free market economy. He then states that these values are now threatened by non-western nations which have different values, Islam being only one of those threats. He makes a point of discussing China's Confucian culture as an example of a nation which holds different values and one which might emerge as a strategic threat. This narrative that "western values" are under siege by foreign nations and cultures is precisely the basis for the present discussion of the "new authoritarianism" and the demonizing of China and Russia.

Oligarchical Values

One of the greatest difficulties in refuting the arguments arising from the Clash of Civilizations thesis is that many well educated individuals accept—uncritically—the axiomatic view that European and American culture is based on "human rights, liberal democracy, and the capitalist free market economy." This view is not only hegemonic among American elites; it is believed by many prominent people from China, Japan, the Islamic world, and elsewhere, particularly those who were educated at American and British universities.

Samuel P. Huntington, author of the 1996 book, The Clash of Civilizations.

But it is not true.

In reality, the American Revolution was waged against what the *London Telegraph* and other sewer press today proclaim as Western Values, and Americans are being asked today to buy into a British-created-and-directed confrontation with Russia and China in direct opposition to the founding principles of their own nation.

In 1763, with the Treaty of Paris—which ended the Seven Years War between Britain and France—the British Empire emerged victorious as the hegemonic power throughout the planet, a position it would maintain well into the 20th Century. This was the same Empire that was the leading slave-trading power in the world, the leading narcotics trafficker, and the very Empire which, in India,

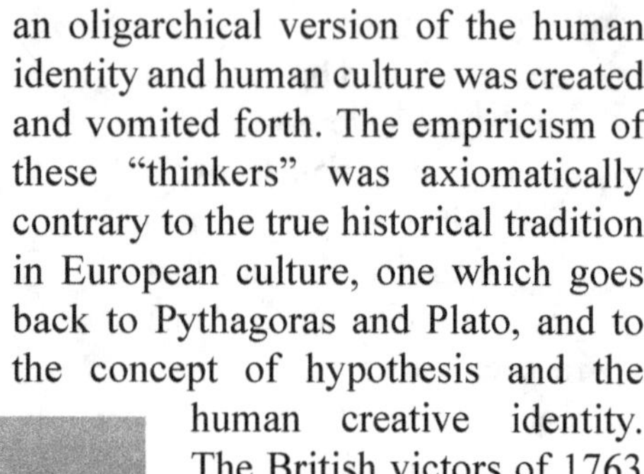

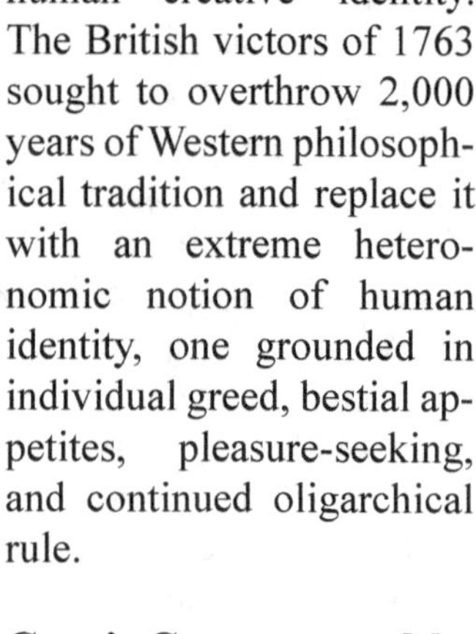

British East India Company victims in Asia. East India Company coat of arms above.

Africa and elsewhere, killed far, far more people than Adolph Hitler—all done out in the open.

Incredibly, it is the philosophical outlook and the political practices of that murderous empire which form the basis of what is today proclaimed as "Western Values."

While the British Empire was murdering tens of millions, it was also developing new forms of oligarchical rule. This became known as "British Liberalism." Britain was a *liberal* empire, one which embraced Whig principles of free trade and parliamentary rule. As is evident in Jeremy Bentham's Hedonistic (*felicific*) Calculus, and the dictum of Adam Smith to "pursue pleasure and avoid pain," it was also an empire which encouraged even the most degenerate forms of "human freedom."

These are not "Western Values"—they are the values of the militarily victorious British Empire, the values of the propagandists for the British East India Company. Through the writings of Francis Bacon, Thomas Hobbes, John Locke, David Hume, Adam Smith, Parson Malthus, Jeremy Bentham, and others,

an oligarchical version of the human identity and human culture was created and vomited forth. The empiricism of these "thinkers" was axiomatically contrary to the true historical tradition in European culture, one which goes back to Pythagoras and Plato, and to the concept of hypothesis and the human creative identity. The British victors of 1763 sought to overthrow 2,000 years of Western philosophical tradition and replace it with an extreme heteronomic notion of human identity, one grounded in individual greed, bestial appetites, pleasure-seeking, and continued oligarchical rule.

Cusa's Commonwealth

In 1433, at the time of the great Council of Florence, Cardinal Nicholas of Cusa, writing in Book II of his *Concordantia Catholica*, states,

> Since Natural Law is based on reason, all law by nature is rooted in the reason of man.

and later in Book III of the same work, he says:

> There is in the people a divine seed by virtue of their common equal birth and the equal natural rights of all men, so that all authority—which comes from God as does man himself—is recognized as divine when it arises from the common consent of all the subjects . . . This is that divinely ordained marital state of spiritual union based on a lasting harmony by which a commonwealth is guided in the fullness of peace toward eternal bliss.

Twelve years after the conclusion of the Council of Florence, in 1461, Louis XI ascended the throne of France, and proceeded to establish the first modern sovereign nation-state, based on Cusa's Commonwealth

cc/Nick in exsillo

Cardinal Nicholas of Cusa.

King Louis XI of France.

principle.[1] Louis proceeded to build ports, roads, schools, printing houses, industry, and infrastructure. He provided support for the cities, created a national currency, and broke the power of the feudal baronies. These are Louis' own words, taken from his book **Le Rosier des Guerres** (The Rosebush of Wars):

> Considering that the characteristic of Kings and Princes and their Knights, is that their estate and vocation is to defend the common good, both ecclesiastic and secular, and to uphold justice and peace among their subjects, and to do good, they will have good in this world and in the other, and out of doing evil will only come grief; and one must count one day on leaving this world to go and give an account of one's undertakings and receive one's reward. And to expose their lives for others, of which among all other estates of the world is most to be praised and honored. And because the common good which concerns many, which is the public matter of the Realm, is more praiseworthy than the particular, by which the common good is often frustrated; we have gladly put in writing the deeds of princes and of their knights and all the good tenets that served their cause....

The usage of the term Commonwealth has been corrupted and mis-defined over time, but the original concept of Cusa—and the idea put into practice by Louis XI—is that of the Common Good or Greater Good, a principle fully coherent with the American revolutionary idea of the General Welfare. This is not merely a "political" policy; it stems from a recognition of the divine creative potential which exists within each human individual. It is defined by the concept of Man and of Natural Law given by Cusa in the above-cited work.

This is the outlook on the human identity and human society which, in European society, goes back to the Socratic Dialogues of Plato and the Promethean view of Man, the Fire-Bringer found in Aeschylus. This heritage is the only truthful, lawful basis on which to begin a discussion of Western Values. Anything else is utterly fraudulent.

The American Identity

It is time for thinking Americans to begin to seriously consider what has been lost in our own culture. Some of that knowledge, that heritage, is still there, buried as a memory in the consciousness of millions of citizens. But the pride which men and women of previous generations took in their sense of identity—pride in being an American—is increasingly ebbing away. For many born after the assassinations of Martin Luther King, and John and Robert Kennedy, the concept of a distinct, positive American identity is non-existent. It is past time to correct this.

The creation of America was a victory for all humanity, which brought into physical existence a nation and a national culture based on Cusa's Commonwealth principle—a nation with a noble view of the human individual and one which is Constitutionally bound to the

---

1. "The Commonwealth of France's Louis XI: Foundations of the Nation State," by Pierre Beaudry, *New Federalist*, July 3, 1995.

principle of upward human progress.

Years ago, the term "melting pot" was used to describe the process whereby immigrant families were assimilated, over several generations, into a higher culture, one based on universal principles, superior to the oligarchical cultures from which they had fled. America represented an ideal—a potential—of what human society could become, and it was that vision of America which Martin Luther King devoted his life to rescuing.[2]

This notion of a distinct American identity is not an academic exercise. If we are to successfully resist the efforts of the British Crown to drag us into a global confrontation with Russia and China, it is of critical importance that we begin with a full comprehension of the deep philosophical and moral gulf which separates the history of the United States from that of the British Empire. Only then will American citizens be able to resist the lies in the news media and the barrage of propaganda now being thrown against us.

Oligarchic Principles

It is suggested here that readers of this article from China, Japan, India, Russia, and elsewhere reflect for a moment on the history of their own cultures. There are periods from the history of every nation—sometimes lasting centuries—that many people would like to forget, periods of decline, retrogression, and oligarchical rule. Yet the values which ruled society during those "bad eras" do not represent the true character of those nations, nor their people. Such is the case with the era of British Liberalism.

With the 1601-1609 creation of the Dutch Empire, an Amsterdam-based laboratory was established for the purpose of creating a new empirical "science," one which would justify the outlook and practices of a

John Locke

global oligarchical empire. Many of today's speculative financial practices were invented there; the beginning of the concept of "parliamentary democracy" is another product of that era.

René Descartes, Hugo Grotius, and others postulated a new radical materialism and an empirical approach. They abolished the concept of the Greater Good, as well as the *agapic* notion of human creativity. They reduced the human identity to the Hobbesian concept of a war of "each against all," and they postulated a social system based on permanent competition among heteronomic individuals, motivated entirely by appetites, passions, and greed.

In the 1660s, a pair of brothers—Johann and Pieter de la Court—became leading advisors to the Dutch government, authoring many works. In *Political Balance* they write, "Descartes and Hobbes show the way to the theory that should occupy mankind, as he was and not as the old-fashioned professors chose to see him." In the *Political Discourses*, they say, "The natural state is the Hobbesian unrestrained state of nature; the best state exists where the unreasonable passions are most restrained. That is the democratic republic."

For the mouthpieces of the Dutch Empire, democracy is thus defined as a state of animalistic competition among antagonistic human individuals, each governed by his or her own passions and desires, and only restrained by the "rule of law." This is what the oligarchy calls a Republic.

After the Dutch invasion of England in 1688, this anti-human outlook was imported into London. At the same time, between 1688 and 1698 all of the financial and maritime practices of Amsterdam were grafted onto London, with the creation of the Bank of England, the Stock Exchange and the newly rechartered East India Company.

Then, over roughly the next 100 years, a series of writers, including John Locke, Bernard Mandeville,

---

2. See "Martin Luther King's American Presidency" by Dennis Speed, *EIR*, March 30, 2018.

Adam Smith and others, would refine the philosophical axioms for the new Empire. Today, it is the plagiarist and Dutch agent John Locke who is lionized as the primary influence in the development of modern western "democratic values," when, in reality, he was a spokesman for the murderous policies of the new British Empire.

Two of Locke's most famous works are his *Essay Concerning Human Understanding* (of notorious *tabula rasa* fame) and *The Two Treatises of Government*. In the former, he attempts to overthrow the entirety of the positive thread in the history of Western Culture from Plato

Benjamin Franklin

through Cusa. He rejects entirely the reality of human creativity and posits an extreme materialism based on sense-perception. Locke simply denies everything that is truthful about the Human Mind. In the *Two Treatises*, cribbing from a variety of oligarchical scribblers who preceded him, Locke puts forward a bizarre reinterpretation of the *Book of Genesis*, stating:

> At the beginning of mankind's existence, the Law man was under, was rather for APPROPRIATING. God Commanded, and his wants forced him to LABOUR. That was his PROPERTY which could not be taken from him where-ever he had fixed it. And hence subduing or cultivating the Earth, and having Dominion, we see are joined together. The one gave Title to the other. So that God, by commanding to subdue, gave Authority so far to *Appropriate* ... [which] necessarily introduces *Private Possessions*.

This is Locke's *Social Contract* theory: "We are all beasts; we are all governed by Hobbesian passions; we simply have to find a means to live together, without killing one another."

Locke was also the first British proponent of extreme monetarism, wherein the power of money becomes the defining governing principle in society, enforced by the "rule of law." It is this subjugation of society to a system governed by monetary value and individual greed, as posed by Locke, and subsequently developed much further by Adam Smith and others, which forms the basis for what the London *Telegraph* and others today call the Western Value of "liberal economics.'

Constitutional Presidential Government

The good of man cannot consist in the mere pleasures of sense; because when any one of those objects which you love is absent, or cannot be come at, you are certainly miserable; and if the faculty be impaired, though the object be present, you cannot enjoy it ...

I have showed you what it ["the good"] is not. It is not sensual but rational and moral good. It is doing all the good we can to others, by acts of humanity, friendship, generosity, and benevolence; this is that constant and durable good, which will afford contentment and satisfaction always alike, without variation, and diminution.

> Benjamin Franklin, *Dialogue between Philocles and Horatio, Concerning Virtue and Pleasure* (1730)

The issue of government is not one of form, but of *essence*. As the *Preamble* to the *Constitution* of the United States proclaims its intention, a new government is being established "to form a more perfect Union, establish Justice, insure domestic Tranquility, provide for the common defence, promote the general Welfare, and secure the Blessings of Liberty to ourselves and our Posterity."

Unlike the hedonistic outlook of the British aristocracy, the United States of America was created with an *intention*, one identical in nature to Cusa's concept of the Commonwealth. It is grounded in the principle of the Greater Good, and it is defined by a commitment to the General Welfare and the Posterity of the nation.

This also provokes an examination of economic and financial policy. London now accuses China of "Market Authoritarianism," because of the direct role of the Chinese government in the Belt and Road Initiative and the deployment of the banking system to build infrastructure, rail lines and other magnificent projects. Yet, the Chinese approach is completely Hamiltonian! Read Alexander Hamilton's *Report on a National Bank* and his *Report on the Subject of Manufactures*. Hamilton created the concept of National Public Credit as a vital feature of the anti-oligarchical Constitutional American Republic. To deploy Credit and other financial means to deliberately advance the nation, to uplift the people and to create a better future—this is an American policy. It is directly the opposite of British imperial "liberal economics," but it is fully coherent with what China is doing today.

America is also a *Presidential* nation. Unlike most of the European nations, America has never been ruled by a parliamentary system. In truth, what Chatham House and the Council on Foreign Relations proclaim as "western democracy" is a chimera. Parliamentary systems—all of them—are oligarchical systems—weak, ineffectual, easily manipulated and overthrown, while the real power lies outside of the government in the financial elite and their *fondi*, who impose their own degenerate policies and culture on the rest of us.

"Liberal Democracy," as defined by Samuel Huntington, Allister Heath, and others is nothing less than a dictatorship of the financial elite. Their banking, trade and cultural axioms of policy are sacrosanct, and their continued rule is taken for granted, while Parliamentary "democracy" is maintained as pure Kabuki Theater—stylized ritual meant to entertain and distract. This has been the great tragic fate of modern-day Europe, where, despite many heroic and brilliant indi-

Lord John Somers

viduals, oligarchical rule has never been broken.

All of the British-centered tripe about "liberal Parliamentary democracy" goes back to the 1688 British *Declaration of Rights*, written by Lord John Somers. In reality, that Parliamentary "democracy" was precisely the system which was put in place with the creation of the Bank of England and the East India Company, in order to create a system of government which would be subservient to the power and practices of Empire then being imported from Amsterdam.

In the summer of 1787, Alexander Hamilton and Gouverneur Morris crafted the American Presidential system, the which was then put into practice during the eight-year George Washington Presidency. Again—take note!—the key is in the *intention*, not simply the form. Morris and Hamilton recognized that their intended Presidency would establish a means whereby the principles of the Constitution's *Preamble*—as well as those from the *Declaration of Independence*—would be "made flesh," that is, personified in the Office of the Presidency. The American Presidency is a *principle*, not simply an elected office; it is the responsibility of the President to personify the Republic's mission and to honor and further the nation's commitment to the Greater Good.

Ask yourself: Isn't this precisely what we are witnessing today in the thinking and the actions of President Putin of Russia and President Xi of China? Are their actions not governed by an unshakable moral drive to uplift and advance the conditions of their own people? Is this not coherent with the same principle of the General Welfare as defined in our own Constitution?[3] Yes, there are cultural and political differences between America, China and Russia, but it is precisely the possibility that these "Three Presidents"—Putin, Trump, and Xi—might succeed in the creation of a global system based on peace, coopera-

---

3. For an insight into the mission of the Russian President, watch the documentary *Putin*.

The belief in truth has been disappearing in modern U.S.-European culture. Here, a populist women's march in Washington, D.C., 2017.

tion, and economic development, which is driving the British nuts.

Hence, all three Presidents are labeled "authoritarian" by the trans-Atlantic media. The truth is that they simply will no longer abide by the financial and policy dictates of London and Wall Street.

Who Are the Real Authoritarians?

After World War II, a great deal of noise was made about the concept of the *Authoritarian Personality.* Theodore Adorno wrote a book of the same name. Hannah Arendt and many others pontificated on the subject. Little known today, is that many of their collective polemics were aimed at destroying the memory and the policies of Franklin Roosevelt in the right-wing turn under Harry Truman.

Essentially what Arendt—the mistress of the Nazi Martin Heidegger—and others said, is that if you try to assert that you know the Truth about anything, you are an authoritarian personality, perhaps even a Hitler in

the making. There is no truth. There is only opinion.

It should go without saying that Plato would not agree with this. Nor would Kepler, Cusa, Leibniz, Einstein or Lyndon LaRouche. The true history of Western Civilization is made up of individuals such as these, those whose lives were and are committed to discovering truthful principles about the universe and the human identity. But for Arendt and her ilk, they are all authoritarian personalities.

This is the kernel of the fraud about "Western Values." Beginning with operations such as the Princeton Radio Project and the post-World War II founding of the Congress for Cultural Freedom, a new liberal culture of irrational "personal freedom" was proposed in which truth is outlawed. Only opinion is allowed. This is not a "Western Value"; it is an attempt to destroy the actual Western cultural tradition going back to Plato, to destroy the actual human identity of lawful—and truthful—creativity.

Where does that leave us? With a society based on cultural relativism in which anything is allowed. Today, there are many—particularly among today's dumbed-down youth—who are adamant that legalized drug use and addiction are a legitimate component of a society committed to "human freedom." Welcome to Jeremy Bentham's Hedonistic Calculus. Actually, what now exists in the trans-Atlantic world is a crushing culture of conformity, albeit one in which a delicatessen of exotic dishes is permitted. This is all the product of decades of practice at manipulating public opinion by the financial elites.

London's "Western Values" of *liberal democracy,* liberal economics and *personal freedom* have nothing to do with the principles which created and built Western Civilization. Neither are they the basis for the American Republic. What London proclaims as Western Values is what Mozart condemned to the pit in *Don Giovanni.*

If we are to survive and to move forward, our orientation must be to work with President Xi and President Putin to build a better world, including a more hopeful, optimistic world for the children now being born into it. Breakthroughs in science, great physical economic projects which transform the world and uplift the people, and a mission to explore and colonize our Solar system are the necessary future for all of mankind Russia and China are our natural, lawful partners in that great project.

Aldo Moro and 40 Years of an Idea that Could Not Be Murdered

by Claudio Celani

Il Puzzle Moro (The Moro Puzzle)
by Giovanni Fasanella.
Milan: Chiarelettere, 2018.
Paperback: Euro 14.96.

April 2—This year marks the 40th anniversary of the kidnapping and murder of Italian statesman Aldo Moro by the terrorist Red Brigades group. Moro's death was a watershed in Italian and Mediterranean politics, with implications for global East-West and North-South relations. After four decades, the truth about Moro's assassination has not yet fully come out. However, the official version, which holds that the motivations for Moro's elimination must be sought in Italian domestic politics, and that the Red Brigades was an entirely "Italian" phenomenon, is slowly but relentlessly crumbling.

In recent years, two factors have done the most to help excavate the truth on the Moro case: the investigations undertaken by journalist and author Giovanni Fasanella and, most recently, the work of the Parliamentary Investigative Committee on the Moro case— the third such committee—which presented its final report on December 15, 2017. Whereas the Committee established that, contrary to "the truth that could be uttered" publicly, Moro's assassins had international connections and support, Fasanella, for his part, has dug out from British and U.S. archives, documents that demonstrate a British, French, American and Soviet Russian mobilization to stop Moro's policy, with the British pulling the string of a "subversive" solution as an alternative to a traditional *coup d'état*.

Fasanella's latest book, *Il Puzzle Moro* (The Moro

Puzzle), which hit the newsstands and bookstores a few days before the March 16 anniversary of Moro's kidnapping, is both a summary of the Committee's conclusions and an update of Fasanella's earlier works, with additional declassified U.S. and British documents also included.

The book also has the merit of describing Moro's strategic policy in greater depth than the simplification offered by mainstream media. Moro's design was not just to "unblock" the Italian political situation by helping the Italian Communist Party to break with Moscow and fully accept Italy's treaty obligations in the Western Alliance: for such a policy served a larger design to strengthen Italy's natural leadership role in the Mediterranean, using its culture and its industrial potential to favor dialogue and development among all the countries of the Northern African littoral and Southwest Asia.

As Prime Minister in 1963-68, then Foreign Minister 1969-72 and 1973-74, and again Prime Minister 1974-76, Moro had led Italy to play such a leadership role in the Mediterranean, at the same time that French and British colonial powers were surrendering and withdrawing from the newly independent nations of Africa and Southwest Asia. Moro was continuing the policy inaugurated by industrialist Enrico Mattei, who had established "win-win" economic relations with oil-producing countries, thus projecting a new image of the Italian nation and its leadership born out of the antifascist Resistance.

Fasanella correctly identifies the intellectual matrix of such a policy in the great Pope Paul VI, who had been a mentor of Moro's and of the other young leaders who, during the war, had founded the Christian Demo-

Paul VI with Colombians, August 1968.

cratic Party. In 1967, Paul VI issued his encyclical letter, *Populorum Progressio,* a milestone in the history of the Catholic Social Doctrine. For the first time, an authoritative document dealt with injustice not just within a society, but among nations, and specifically between North and South.

"In that letter," Fasanella writes, "the Pope picked up and developed the lines drawn by his predecessor in the Vatican II Council, bringing the social doctrine of the Church to the highest point of its exposure, both of 'technocracies' responsible for starvation, and of neo-colonialism. Each word 'carved' by Paul VI sounded like a whip-lash (*staffilata*) against rich countries and their establishments: 'The progressive development of peoples is an object of deep interest and concern to the Church. This is particularly true in the case of those peoples who are trying to escape the ravages of hunger, poverty, endemic disease and ignorance; of those who are seeking a larger share in the benefits of civilization and a more active improvement of their human qualities; of those who are consciously striving for fuller growth.' And further: 'Colonizing nations were sometimes concerned with nothing save their own interests, their own power and their own prestige,' their oligarchies 'enjoy the refinements of life,' whereas oppressed people 'subsist in living and working conditions unworthy of the human person.'"

The right wing attacked the encyclical as "Marxist," but Paul VI, writes Fasanella, "offered to developing countries a model that was neither predatory capitalism nor oppressive communism. At the same time he broadened the horizon of the Church, overcoming the narrow European context in which it had thus far operated. The negative reaction in Great Britain and in some American and French circles was understandable: the religious influence of the Vatican in Latin America, Africa, and even in some Asian countries was growing at the same pace as Italy's economic influence, while the world around was tumultuously changing, and colonial empires had inexorably come to an end."

In part, using declassified reports and diplomatic wires from UK archives, Fasanella shows that this policy, which Paul VI's friend and disciple Moro had successfully carried out, was the underlying reason that Great Britain set in motion a plan to stop Moro at any cost, first considering the option of a traditional *coup d'état*, but eventually rejecting that in favor of "another option" which, many elements indicate, was Moro's assassination.

Since Moro wanted to involve the Italian Communist Party (PCI) in government responsibilities in order to ensure parliamentary support for his policy, the British used this angle to win U.S. support for their plots. But

Luigi Berlinguer (left) greeting Aldo Moro.

whereas the United States was primarily concerned that Italy not slide into the Soviet sphere of influence—in particular, this was Henry Kissinger's obsession—and therefore the U.S. intent was simply to keep the PCI away from power, the British target was Moro himself. Ultimately, the United States favored a strong Italian role in the Mediterranean as long as Italy stayed in NATO.

On the other hand, the French shared the British concern in their effort to turn back the clock of history. Under the pretext of containing the PCI in Italy, a "directorate" of four countries was created in 1974 among the UK, the United States, France, and Germany—the latter for strategic reasons, given its role in NATO—whose leaders would meet secretly, often in the British embassy in Rome, to plot a "solution" to stop what looked like an unstoppable growth of the PCI, which would predictably soon win a general election, and legitimately claim the national government.

Flashback: In September 1978, a few months after the assassination of Moro, the Partito Operaio Europeo (POE), which represented the LaRouche movement in Italy at the time, published a special report entitled *Chi ha ucciso Aldo Moro?* (Who Killed Aldo Moro?), exposing London as the string-puller of Moro's murder, and identifying the strategic setting and the motivations for the murder in the global fight defined by *Populorum Progressio*.

In our pamphlet, we wrote:

Paul VI's policy clashed with London in all its essential aspects. When London, through its agents, pushed the U.S. to escalate the Vietnam War, Paul VI launched his pilgrimage for peace in New York, at the United Nations. When the British wanted to exploit the coming economic crisis to crush the Third World under the genocidal policy of the International Monetary Fund, Paul VI answered by appointing new cardinals able to express the needs of the Third World as mirrored in his masterpiece, the encyclical *Populorum Progressio*, the manifesto of a new era of economic and cultural development in the former colonies.

At that time, LaRouche's collaborators did not have access to British archives, and their documents had not yet been declassified. Nevertheless, we were able to precisely identify the apparatus that killed Aldo Moro by locating Moro's and Paul VI's fight for development in

Prime Minister Moro with U.S. Secretary of State Henry Kissinger in 1974.

the continuity of the fight against the oligarchy, represented in modern times by the British Empire. The oligarchical apparatus was visible to anyone who wanted to see it, but political forces and institutions were blinded by the "left-right" game of conventional politics.

The POE dossier contained some flaws, such as, for instance, a wrong assessment of Soviet policy, as well as a misunderstanding of the efforts by some forces in Italy to negotiate with the Red Brigades for Moro's freedom. In recent decades such aspects have been clarified, thanks to investigations conducted by Fasanella and others. But the POE dossier indicated the right direction to follow, and its insightful work was early acknowledged by the Parliamentary Committees and by serious investigators.

Moro and Libya, Malta, Tunisia, Iraq

The Moro Puzzle starts at the end of World War II, when Britain arranged that Italy, although it had joined the Allied Forces in the last phase of the war, should not be admitted to the peace talks and should not be allowed to have a future security and foreign policy of its own.

It was none other than Winston Churchill who explained the British doctrine to the Apostolic Nuncio in Britain in November 1945. Although no longer Prime Minister, Churchill's role in the British and international establishment was still important. The content of the conversation is found in the U.S. National Archives. Churchill told the Pope's envoy that the United States and the USSR considered the Italian question to be under "British competence," thus recognizing a sort of supervision over the country by London. As Great Britain performed this function, the United States would give "every possible moral and material" support to Rome, "but in the framework of British interests." As for the Soviet Union, Moscow would "leave Italy totally in peace," thus doing nothing to help the Italian Communist Party take power.

Within that agreement, Moscow and Washington shared the British reservation: "the only thing that Italy won't have is a full political freedom" for "many years." "Political control will be exerted as discretely as possible," but the Pope should already know that London had some "doubts" about "some left-wing factions in the Christian Democratic party."

Political events in postwar Italy must be read under the light of that statement. Leaders who threatened to escape such control were eliminated physically, like the industrialist Enrico Mattei, or politically, as was Alcide De Gasperi's designated successor as leader of the Christian Democratic (DC) party in 1954. (For an extensive treatment of the Mattei case, see: http://www.larouchepub.com/eiw/public/2009/eirv36n22-20090605/eirv36n22-20090605_044-_mattei_and_kennedy_the_strategic.pdf).

"There is a constant in the entire history of Italy as a nation-state, which looks like a curious paradox, if not a real curse: each time that Italy aspires to play a major role on the international scene, the rate of internal squabbling increases and dries out energies, resources, and projects. And ultimately forces you to get back in line," Fasanella writes.

Nevertheless, with a dirigistic economic policy led by De Gasperi, Mattei and Moro, Italy succeeded in an unprecedented post-war economic recovery and was increasingly playing its natural role of leadership in the Mediterranean. Fasanella cites documents from the British Foreign Office and British diplomats expressing concern about Moro's foreign policy that attracted countries such as Libya, Egypt and even Malta into what the British saw as a growing "sphere of influence," at the same time that Britain's own military bases were being kicked out of those nations.

Moro probably crossed a red line when, in 1966, he reorganized the NATO "Stay Behind" network in Italy. According to Fasanella's sources, Moro pulled the "Stay Behind" organization (Gladio) out of British con-

wikipedia

Shattered interior of the Banca Nazionale dell'Agricoltura, after the bombing of the Piazza Fontana, Milan, 1969.

trol, and put it under joint U.S.-Italian control. The British network then created the "Armed Nuclei for the Defense of the State" out of a former Gladio section, under its main asset in Italy, Count Edgardo Sogno Rata del Vallino. Sogno was eventually used for organizing an attempted *coup d'état*—eventually cancelled—and to steer the Red Brigades. Although the Red Brigades terrorist organization was fabricated from radical elements left over from the communist faction of the Resistance, which felt "betrayed" by the constitutional shift adopted by the Communist Party in 1944, British intelligence networks played a role in taking over the organization, directing it in the phase that led to the kidnapping and assassination of Moro. (See: http://www.larouchepub.com/eiw/public/2005/eirv32n03-20050121/eirv32n03-20050121_054-the_sphinx_and_the_gladiators_ho.pdf)

The terrorist destabilization of Italy started in 1969, with the Milan Piazza Fontana bombings, and ended in 1978 with the assassination of Moro. The British themselves named this phase "the Strategy of Tension." The fictive or real threat of a right-wing coup was used to create a leftist insurgency, which produced the Red Brigades and other terrorist groups, escalating into the

The scene of the Aldo Moro kidnapping, where his five bodyguards were killed.

large insurgency of the "Armed Party" centered around Autonomia Operaia in 1977.

In 1976, the British set up a Committee of 15 Foreign Office and Defense officials, which produced a report considering two options for Italy: either a classical military coup, or, as the fallback option, "support for a different subversive action." Fasanella had already published the relevant British documents in his book *Il Golpe Inglese* (The British Coup). (See: http://www.larouchepub.com/eiw/public/2011/eirv38n38-20110930/20-24_3838.pdf) In *The Moro Puzzle*, Fasanella brings in new documents which detail how the report was first discussed with the United States and Germany, which opposed a coup, and was then re-drafted to take account of their concerns, but leaving open Option B.

A few months later, Alan Hugh Campbell, the head of the "Fifteen" committee that had drafted the paper, was sent to Rome to replace the British Ambassador, to implement the "different action."

The "different action" was probably the use of the Red Brigades, said Claudio Signorile in a recent interview. Signorile had been charged by then Socialist leader Bettino Craxi to establish contact with the Red Brigades to negotiate Moro's freedom.

Moro was kidnapped on March 16 and kept in captivity for 55 days. During those agonizing 55 days, while all political forces officially shared the line that there should be no negotiations with the terrorists, several attempts were made unofficially to contact the Red Brigades and negotiate Moro's freedom, including one by Socialist leader Bettino Craxi, and one by Pope Paul VI himself, who had prepared one billion lire (the equivalent of one million euro today) as a ransom. Italy's President Giovanni Leone was ready to sign a pardon for a jailed terrorist, and on the evening of May 8, everything was ready for Amintore Fanfani, a Christian Democratic (DC) leader and ally of Moro, to intervene at the DC leadership meeting the next day and announce the decision.

Instead, on that morning of May 9, the Red Brigades communicated that they had executed Aldo Moro, and his corpse was to be found in a red Renault 4 in Via Caetani, in the center of Rome—around the corner from both the DC and the PCI headquarters.

Fasanella's book advances the hypothesis that the negotiations failed because, at one point, a third party came in and "took over" the hostage from the Red Brigades. In previous books, such as *Il Misterioso Intermediario*, Fasanella has detailed the role that Hubert Howard—a British intelligence officer who had married into the aristocratic Caetani family and was living in the Palazzo Caetani in Via Caetani—might have had in that final phase of Moro's captivity, including giving the assassination order.

In *The Moro Puzzle*, Fasanella reports that in 2008, the late President of Italy, Francesco Cossiga, who was police minister before and during Moro's kidnapping, revealed to him that NATO had taken over police opera-

Italian President Francesco Cossiga (left) with Aldo Moro.

tions during Moro's captivity, fearing that Moro could reveal sensitive NATO secrets to his captors. "NATO took the situation into its hands through special Stay Behind units and through Germany, which at that time was leading the directorate that coordinated Atlantic intelligence services." This was revealed in an official BND (West German intelligence service) document in 1990, which Cossiga had received and forwarded to prosecutors—but only after having deleted mention of the Stay Behind.

One month after its publication, *The Moro Puzzle* is already in its third printing. Fasanella is holding conferences every other day throughout Italy. This is a good sign, and leads one to hope that at some point, this will be reflected in a political shift.

The lessons of history drawn from *The Moro Puzzle* are evident if one looks at contemporary events. Two examples: the war against Libya in 2011, and the Regeni case, which provoked a crisis between Italy and Egypt in 2016.

The Libyan war was launched by then French President Nicolas Sarkozy, backed by the British government, the United States, and NATO, one year after Italy had signed a friendship treaty with Libya, in which Italy recognized its past responsibilities as colonial invader, and committed itself to reparations in the form of major infrastructure. The result of the Anglo-French-American war and the assassination of Qaddafi has been the destruction of the Libyan state and the spreading of terrorism, including Libyan weapons and militias flowing into Syria. Italy not only lost a major trading partner and oil supplier, but has suffered the greatest burden of the wave of refugees.

In Egypt, Italian student Giulio Regeni was found dead in February 2016 in Cairo, and as a result of a campaign by Amnesty International accusing Egyptian President Al-Sisi, the Italian Renzi government withdrew its Ambassador, who was not sent back for more than a year. In fact, Regeni had been set up by his Cambridge University tutor, an anti-Sisi activist, who gave

The Anglo-French-American-led NATO war against Libya shattered the Libya-Italy friendship treaty.

Regeni a highly dangerous mission. His body was delivered the same day that a high-level economic delegation from Italy, led by the industry minister, was visiting Cairo, and after ENI, the Italian national oil company, had discovered the largest gas field ever found in the Mediterranean, which would make Egypt self-sufficient in energy.

Italy was pushed out of Libya and out of Egypt, albeit temporarily, but long enough to prevent the possibility of a stabilizing role for Italy in Libya together with Egypt, itself backed by Russia. Although the Italian Ambassador is back in Cairo and some of the mistakes have been exposed, it is still difficult today for Italy to find national unity behind a policy. As Fasanella wrote, in crucial moments when unity is needed, "the rate of squabbling increases" among political factions. The result of the last general elections is exemplary: No party won a majority, and it seems easier to climb Mount Everest than to find common ground for a coalition.

And yet, the small action undertaken at the end of February by the outgoing Italian government in Abuja, Nigeria, shows the way Italy can rally national support behind a the pursuit of Moro's and Paul VI's design. As a result of years of organizing by the Schiller Institute and this author in particular, a grand design for Africa took its first step when it was announced that, thanks to an Italian grant, the feasibility study for the Transaqua project will finally begin (see http://www.larouchepub.com/eiw/private/2018/2018_10-19/2018-10/pdf/06-13_4510.pdf).

Although a small step in terms of resources, this decision has great political significance, as international media quickly realized. Italy is the first European nation to take a concrete step in cooperation with China for the development of Africa, in the true spirit of the Belt and Road. This is just the beginning, but the dynamic is unstoppable. As Giovanni Fasanella writes in the conclusion of his book, "history is patient and always takes its revenge."

Court Decision Covers for British Hand Behind 9/11

by Barbara Boyd

April 2—On March 29, 2018, U.S. District Judge George Daniels was forced to provide—to the surviving relatives of the 2,996 individuals murdered at the World Trade Center on September 11, 2001, and the more than 6,000 injured on that day—limited discovery about the perpetrators of that crime.

The Judge's hand was forced by JASTA, the Justice Against Sponsors of Terrorism Act, passed by the U.S. Congress in 2016 over President Obama's veto. JASTA allowed the 9/11 families, for the first time in over sixteen years, to add the Kingdom of Saudi Arabia as a defendant in their lawsuit seeking redress for the 9/11 attacks. Saudi Arabia has been protected by provisions of U.S. laws shielding foreign sovereign nations from U.S. lawsuits, as well as by the Bush family, Dick Cheney, and U.S. intelligence agencies, themselves implicated in the events of 9/11. Fifteen of the nineteen hijackers were Saudi nationals who arrived in the United States well prior to the attack, and lived and trained here. Prominent in this cover-up is Robert S. Mueller III, the Special Prosecutor whose present as-signment is to take out the President of the United States.

While the families were tossed a significant morsel by a Judge whose hostility otherwise shines through his March 29 decision, the crime at issue here was monstrous. Moreover, in any just society, the treatment of these families by their government, as they sought justice for their murdered loved ones, would have resulted in popular revulsion and outrage, a very, very long time ago.

In the Kafkaesque cover-up directed at these families, the government first sought to buy them off with a Victim's Compensation Fund which provided money damages if they signed away their right to sue any of the airlines involved in 9/11. The families then had to fight the Bush Administration to appoint a Commission to investigate the 9/11 events after the Joint Congressional Committee investigating the events ran out of time, and had 28 pages of its report concerning the Saudis censored by classification on the direct demand of then FBI Director Mueller.

The press conference featuring Sen. Rand Paul's introduction of a Senate resolution, calling for the release of the classified 28 pages of the 9/11 Inquiry Report, June 2, 2016. Former Senator Bob Graham is at the microphone.

The Justice Against Sponsors of Terrorism Act was passed in 2016 over Obama's veto.

Once the families overcame Bush Administration attempts to kill the very idea of an investigative commission, the person originally designated by George Bush to head the Commission was none other than Henry Kissinger. When the families succeeded in disqualifying Kissinger, based on obvious conflicts of interest, Philip Zelikow was inserted, instead, as staff director, controlling the entire investigation.

Zelikow was a Bush Administration insider who had written the Administration's national security documents justifying preemptive war in Iraq. Moreover, the Bush Administration's mandate for the Commission explicitly prevented it from finding fault. Its findings relied on Robert Mueller's fabulously flawed PENTBOM investigation[1] and included false confessions to numerous actions by Khalid Sheikh Mohammed after he was tortured and water-boarded hundreds of times. Zelikow fired the investigator most familiar with Saudi involvement in the attacks and sought to whitewash the Saudi role, inclusive of making last-minute and preposterous claims about Iranian involvement in 9/11. The Saudi chapter was shortened and edited to make way for these last-minute, bogus Iranian claims.

When the families sought to charge Saudi Arabia in court, using the extant doctrines concerning sovereign immunity prior to JASTA, that aspect of their suit was dismissed because Saudi Arabia was not listed by the U.S. State Department as an official state sponsor of terrorism, despite widespread and public acknowledgment of exactly that fact. The Saudis have repeatedly claimed in court that the 9/11 Commission report, written by Zelikow, exonerates them concerning involvement in 9/11, despite affidavits from several Commissioners denying that claim.

In this publication's dossier on Special Counsel Robert S. Mueller III, we urged President Trump to declassify all files concerning the Saudis, the British, and complicit U.S. officials with respect to the events of September 11, 2001 and the obstruction of any real investigation of those events.

Were the President to declassify all of this information, Mueller—who played an absolutely critical role in this cover-up—would stand exposed, having nakedly obstructed justice with regard to the actual events of 9/11. Mueller covered for the Saudis and the Bush Administration while playing an essential role, as FBI Director, in creating the modern U.S. surveillance state, which now engulfs all of us. Creation of the modern Leviathan in which we now live was the result intended by the perpetrators of 9/11. By this single act of declassification, the President would be free of Robert Muel-

---

1. As detailed in *EIR*'s Mueller Dossier, Mueller investigated and endlessly harassed an innocent man, Stephen Hatfill, for the anthrax letter attacks, resulting in a multi-million dollar legal settlement for Hatfill. Mueller barely escaped civil liability himself for rounding up and torturing innocent Muslims in New York during the PENTBOM investigation.

President George W. Bush announces Robert Mueller to be director of the FBI, during an event in the Rose Garden, Thursday, July 5, 2001.

Bernard Lewis

Zbigniew Brzezinski

ler, and the cause of elementary justice on behalf of these families and the nation as a whole would finally be served.

Lyndon LaRouche, in a series of publications before and after 9/11, correctly called 9/11 a Saudi/British operation used by Vice President Dick Cheney and others to destroy the last vestiges of our constitutional form of government. The evidence adduced by the families, the parade of government officials who have attempted to block the viewing of that evidence, and a short overview of Saudi Arabia's complete and total subservience to British geopolitical designs, more than validate this claim.

The Saudis Have Never Been Anything Other Than a British Tool

While recent efforts at reform of Saudi Arabia involving the Russians, the Chinese, and Donald Trump may present a more hopeful prospect for the future, they defy the Kingdom's entire history and most certainly do not represent what the Kingdom was as of September 11, 2001. The Saudi role as a British colonial destabilization and asymmetric warfare tool against other nations in the Middle East was enshrined in the Sykes-Picot agreement in 1916. The Saudi Royal family loyally performed this role against any Arab nationalist eager to develop his country, most notably Gamal Abdel Nasser of Egypt. The British and the United States were equally adept at using Shia Muslim extremists for the

same purpose. In 1953, they used Shia extremists to overthrow Iran's nationalist leader, Mohammad Mosaddegh.

Ayatollah Khomeini's coup against the Shah similarly was an Anglo-American project based on imperial geopolitical designs and on the Shah's anti-British actions to finally fully develop his nation. That coup united Shia extremists with the Muslim Brotherhood.[2]

The immediate roots of 9/11 are to be found in the plotting of Zbigniew Brzezinski and British Islamic expert Bernard Lewis to create an "arc of crisis" by balkanizing the entire Muslim Near East along tribal and religious lines. Under the Bernard Lewis Plan, chaos caused by religious wars in the Arc of Crisis would spill over into Muslim regions of the Soviet Union. Brzezinski takes credit for drawing the Soviet Union into war in Afghanistan by using the radical Salafists constituting the Mujahideen to overthrow the Soviet-friendly regime in Kabul in 1979. His goal was to create a "Viet Nam" for Russia and destabilize Russia's southern border.

Thereafter, successive U.S. and British governments recruited and trained Salafist terrorists from throughout the world to fight their ten-year holy war in Afghanistan, using the Saudis and Pakistan as their

2. For an excellent history of the Saudi/British relationship, see Mark Curtis, *Secret Affairs, Britain's Collusion with Radical Islam* (London: Profile Books, 2010).

Saudi Prince Bandar bin Sultan (left) with British Prime Minister Margaret Thatcher.

main vehicles for recruitment and funding. In addition to direct funding by the Saudis and Pakistan, the Anglo-American Afghanistan operation was financed by turning the country into the world's prime supplier of heroin. This was further complemented by the Al-Yamamah arms-for-oil arrangements negotiated by Margaret Thatcher and Saudi Prince Bandar bin Sultan in 1985, which created a worldwide flow of hot funds supporting terrorism and propping up, at various times, the City of London's bankrupt monetarist apparatus.

When the Anglo-Americans went to war in the Balkans in the 1990s, a whole new front for these sponsored terrorist mercenaries was opened up and funded, for the same British geopolitical goal of targeting and weakening Russia. The British and Saudi royal families are extremely close, and their economies virtually integrated.

Interviewed by *Le Nouvel Observateur*, Brzezinski was asked if he regretted his support of Islamic fundamentalism, given its evolution into terrorism. He said, "What is more important in world history? The Taliban or the collapse of the Soviet empire? Some agitated Moslems or the liberation of Central Europe and the end of the cold war?" It was, of course, precisely these "agitated Moslems" who murdered almost 3,000 Americans on September 11, 2001.

Khalid al-Mihdhar

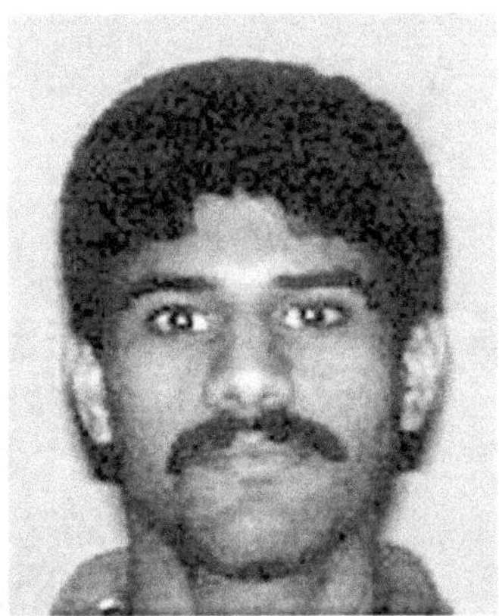

Nawaf al-Hazmi

Omar al-Bayoumi

Fahad al-Thumairy

The New Complaint and the Discovery Decision

The 9/11 families' 2017 post-JASTA Complaint naming the Kingdom of Saudi Arabia as a defendant, provides a detailed map of evidence presently known about the Saudi state role in the 9/11 attack. While limited by years of determined U.S. and British government interference, lies, and overt and vicious official misconduct, the Complaint more than demonstrates Saudi state sponsorship of terrorism culminating in the 9/11 attack on the United States. Any doubts about this will be resolved if you simply read the evidence set forth in their Complaint.[3]

Significant evidence set forth in the Complaint results from the declassification of 28 pages of the Joint Congressional Inquiry report, showing direct Saudi government support of two of the 9/11 hijackers, Nawaf al-Hazmi and Khalid al-Mihdhar, who operated out of San Diego. As previously noted, these 28 pages were formerly suppressed and classified on Robert Mueller's personal order. The FBI reports from which the 28 pages are drawn were viewed by the Joint Congressional Committee staff in San Diego after Mueller explicitly ordered them not to go to San Diego. Former U.S. Senator Robert Graham states that Mueller otherwise "aggressively deceived" the United States Congress in his all-out effort to shield the Saudis and others from legal scrutiny during the Joint Congressional Inquiry.

---

3. See https://28pages.org/2017/04/06/complaint-in-911-suit-reveals-depth-of-case-against-kingdom/

President George W. Bush (left) meeting with Saudi Arabian Ambassador Prince Bandar bin Sultan in Crawford, Texas, Aug. 27, 2002.

Similar obstruction was undertaken by Robert Mueller, Dick Cheney, and other Bush Administration officials on behalf of the other Saudi hijackers and their support networks, most demonstrably in Florida, where thousands of FBI and other intelligence documents remain suppressed and classified to this day. This obstruction began almost immediately after the 9/11 attacks, when numerous Saudi citizens were flown out of the country as the result of a deal between the Bush Administration and Prince Bandar, placing them beyond the reach of any investigation. Bandar, the Saudi Ambassador to the United States, was so close to the Bush family that he was called Bandar Bush in knowledgeable circles.

Nawaf al-Hazmi and Khalid al-Mihdhar were known Al-Qaeda terrorists, carrying passports specially marked by the Saudi government indicating that they were terrorists. They were the first of the 9/11 terrorists to land in the United States and settled in San Diego. Prince Bandar has publicly stated that such terrorists were under precise surveillance by the Saudi government prior to the events of 9/11, and Prince Turki has stated that Hazmi and al-Mihdhar were known Al-Qaeda watch list terrorists as of 1999-2000. The two hijackers received assistance in San Diego from Fahad al-Thumairy, a radical Islamist cleric who worked out of the Saudi Consulate in Los Angeles, and from Omar al-Bayoumi.

Bayoumi was in the United States on a false student visa and had a no-show job with a Saudi government entity, which increased his salary massively once he began assisting the hijackers. The FBI considered Bayoumi to be a Saudi intelligence agent. In San Diego, the hijackers rented an apartment from an FBI informant whose identity and information have been concealed, possibly forever, by Robert Mueller. The assistance provided by Thumairy and al-Bayoumi to the two hijackers included transportation, lodging, communications, social activities, English language and social skills, assimilation, and flight training. During this time, Bayoumi had numerous contacts with the Saudi Arabian Embassy in Washington, D.C., including with diplomat Khalid al-Suwailem, who worked for the Ministry of Islamic Affairs at the Embassy.

Judge Daniels has allowed the families discovery on al-Bayoumi and Thumairy only. They will be allowed discovery to demonstrate the relationship of these two individuals to the Saudi government. There is no apparent rationale for Judge Daniels' decision, since other evidence and targets for discovery were equally compelling.

To cite but a few examples, the families sought discovery on Osama Bassman, Mohammed al-Qudhaeein, Hamdan al-Shalawi, and Saleh al-Hussayen, each of whom had extremely significant relationships with the Saudi government. Bassman bragged to an FBI informant that he had helped the San Diego hijackers even more than al-Bayoumi. While doing so, Bassman and his wife had received direct cash payments from Prince Bandar. Al-Qudhaeein and al-Shalawi, two Saudi students, while flying to Washington for an event at the Saudi Embassy, conducted a dry-run probe of cockpit defenses during their flight.

Al-Hussayen is a senior Saudi cleric who arrived in Virginia shortly before the attacks, and switched his lodging to the hotel which housed the Flight 77 hijackers. Interviewed by the FBI about this, he "passed out or feigned a seizure," was taken to the hospital, and allegedly gave the FBI the slip thereafter. Upon his return to Saudi Arabia, he was promoted and oversaw the holiest sites in Islam, the Mecca and Medina mosques. Judge Daniels disallowed this discovery as well as any discovery concerning the vast Saudi state mechanism for funding terrorism through various Saudi charities.

But the truth will come out.

ZEPP-LAROUCHE WEBCAST

How to Outflank Mad Theresa May's March to World War III

This is the edited transcript of the March 29, 2018 Schiller Institute New Paradigm webcast, an interview with the founder of the Schiller Institutes, Helga Zepp-LaRouche. She was interviewed by Harley Schlanger. A video *of the webcast is available.*

Harley Schlanger: Hello. I'm Harley Schlanger of the Schiller Institute. Welcome to our weekly international strategic webcast, featuring our founder Helga Zepp-LaRouche.

There's been an extraordinary escalation on the part of the British over the last few weeks, to move toward a pre-war situation with Russia. Prime Minister Theresa May has been mobilizing the European governments, putting pressure on the United States, the Commonwealth nations, and others, to get what she's calling a "unified force," to adopt "European values." Now, since when did World War III become a "European value"?

We certainly have to evaluate the situation from the top, with all the danger involved. Helga, I'd like to start with your assessment of what's happened in the last week.

Helga Zepp-LaRouche: It is extremely interesting. You can see who's who, and who is on what side, by the reactions to the British insistence that the only plausible explanation for the Skripal assassination attempt is that Russia is responsible. Let me go through some of the international reactions, which will provide a quite good picture of this.

The Russian Foreign Ministry issued an official statement, stating that unless the British provide concrete proof, Russia would have to conclude that UK intelligence services were involved in the operation, as part of a broad, international provocation against Russia. That is what *we* put out as a hypothesis, immediately, that this whole operation was a new phase of Trumpgate, or Russiagate, or Muellergate, whatever name one might give to the collusion between the Obama administration intelligence heads with British intelligence, to oust President Trump.

At a certain point that operation was falling apart and the investigation in the U.S. Congress was pointing to the role of the British—the collusion with a foreign government was not with Russia, but with the British government. At that point, there were expectations that Theresa May would be out of office any day. Jeremy Corbyn, the leader of the Labour Party, was the rising star in British policy. That's when she pulled this opera-

United Nations Security Council's meeting on the poisoning of former spy Sergei Skripal, March 14, 2018.

Austrian Foreign Minister Karin Kneissl.

tion, which was nothing but an attempt to reset the agenda in the direction of the geopolitical aims of British confrontation against Russia and China.

The fact that the Russian Foreign Ministry is also mooting the possibility of UK intelligence involvement is very interesting. That certainly sheds a bad light on all of those who, without asking any questions and with no proof being presented, immediately fell into line behind Theresa May. Fortunately, this was not so many people. Even though there was the mass expulsion of Russian diplomats from 10 European countries and the United States, the picture as a whole is more differentiated. The Chinese Foreign Ministry denounced the "Cold War mentality" of countries seeking confrontation with Russia. The Chinese Foreign Ministry spokeswoman said this was a tool used by the Europeans and the United States to attempt to achieve unity when they were completely disunited. This is the old geopolitical game: to create unity you create war, and then everyone must fall into line.

The reactions were, however, quite differentiated: Japan refused to expel diplomats, as did New Zealand, which is part of the Five Eyes intelligence alliance of the United States, UK, Canada, Australia, and New Zealand. Greece, Cyprus, Bulgaria, Malta, Slovakia, Slovenia, Luxembourg, and Portugal—I may have forgotten a few nations—all refused to expel any diplomats. The EU unity did not hold. Even in Germany, many voices—representatives of almost all of the par-

ties in the German parliament (the Bundestag)— were against this, including Günter Verheugen, the former SPD EU commissioner; Ralf Stegner, SPD deputy chairman; outgoing foreign minister and former SPD chairman Sigmar Gabriel; Matthias Platzeck, former SPD chairman; Sarah Wagenknecht, co-chairperson of Die Linke; and from the FDP, Bundestag vice president Wolfgang Kubicki. There is very broad rejection of the endorsements of this provocation.

The Austrian government was perhaps the strongest. Austria refused to expel any diplomats, insisting that Austria is a neutral country and regards itself as a bridge between East and West. The Austrian Foreign Minister, Karin Kneissl, said that even if it were proven that Russia had been the perpetrator of this attack, this would not change Austria's position.

If you look at this very broad spectrum of reactions, you can see, actually, that the British provocation and those who are backing it are exposed. We have seen reactions, in our own organizing in the United States and in Europe, that clearly indicate that the people, in general, are not falling for this at all. Most everyone thinks that this is a complete provocation, that there is no proof. It is not going well for the British. This provocation, however, continues to be very dangerous and should continue to be denounced. If the UK doesn't produce any proof, it should be accused of leading an effort to manipulate world public opinion in an outrageous and extremely dangerous way.

So this is a very interesting picture after two weeks.

Schlanger: There were other events which forced their hand. You mentioned the Russiagate falling apart—we'll get back to that in a moment. There are some new developments indicating that the people pushing the whole fraud, are the ones who are now becoming the defendants. There was Putin's "Sputnik Shock" speech on March 1, the March 18 Putin election victory, and then the March 20 Putin discussion with Trump, all of which provide significant momentum for what President Trump said he wanted to do, when he ran for President, namely, to collaborate with Russia. It is in the midst of this that we had the Theresa May operation.

What about France and Germany going along, in lockstep, with Theresa May? What is of interest there?

British Prime Minister Theresa May.

German Chancellor Angela Merkel.

What does that say about the situation within the core EU?

Zepp-LaRouche: The case of France is a bit more complicated, because Macron has had a slightly different emphasis on cooperation with the New Silk Road and China, than Merkel. French Foreign Minister Yves Le Drian has just announced that Macron will go to Moscow in May. That is certainly a bit different than Mrs. Merkel's attitude, which is a shame. This new "Grand Coalition" government is not very grand at all. They are all falling like stones in the polls. This is a reflection of the fact that, presently, there is no German elite worthy of the name.

People in Germany should not accept that, but should instead reflect on the history of the German-Russian relationship. There were two world wars, and the memory of the Second World War is indelibly etched into the memory of every Russian, yet Russia agreed to German re-unification in a peaceful way, without any shots being fired or tanks being deployed. Russia gave up East Germany and agreed to unification, and was given promises at that time that NATO would never be expanded to the borders of Russia. That promise was broken. Then you had all these escalations. So in a certain sense, I can imagine that Russians feel betrayed by this kind of behavior by Merkel.

Merkel has a specific background. Many people keep asking themselves, what makes this woman tick? Nobody has been able to answer that question in any satisfying way. But, I think the Russians do feel betrayed. Germany should go back to the kind of *Ostpolitik* [policy toward the East], at minimum, which was characteristic of the German attitude over an extended period, a good-neighbor policy of peaceful dialogue and cooperation. It is really, really important that people in Germany not fall in line with this aggressive British policy that Merkel is following like a puppy dog. I must, however, say that puppies are cuter than Mrs. Merkel.

But this is a serious matter. People should not fall for this propaganda. This is the kind of thing which could go out of control and trigger a new world war. Who would want that?

Schlanger: The other underlying cause of hysteria from the City of London has been the unstoppable progress of the New Silk Road. There was a conference in Portugal this week, which I know you know something about. A new government in Italy appears to be coming together that will probably not go along with sanctions against Russia. What else can you add about the situation in Europe? Why don't you start with the Portugal situation?

Zepp-LaRouche: This is positive and very good. It confirms what I have been saying for a long time: The New Silk Road initiative is unstoppable; the Spirit of the Silk Road has seized the imagination of a great many nations.

In Lisbon, the Friends of the New Silk Road Association organized a conference which was addressed by the Portuguese Foreign Minister, the Chinese Ambassador, and many other VIPs. There was discussion of making Portugal a hub, not only for the western end of the landline of the New Silk Road, but also to build up the Port of Sines, a deep water port about 200 km south of Lisbon, to extend the high-speed railway from Madrid, Spain to Sines, and turn it into a connection

Xinhua/Zhang Liyun

Portuguese Foreign Minister Augusto Santos Silva speaks at a conference on Portugal's participation in the Belt and Road Initiative in Lisbon, March 23, 2018. Right: the Port of Sines, already one of Europe's busiest.

point between the land Silk Road and the Maritime Silk Road, making this deep water port also a connection to the Portuguese-speaking countries and areas in Africa, Asia, and Latin America.

That is very good. Portugal is taking this approach, and Spain is in the same mode. Italy is working together with China on the Transaqua project in Africa. Greece, Switzerland, Austria, and the 16+1 countries in Central and Eastern Europe, are also joining.

The process is moving forward. The obstructionism which continues to come from the EU in Brussels, as well as from Berlin and London, will be swept aside at a certain point. I think this is very good.

Schlanger: There was another very interesting flank this week, which seems to have once again caught the U.S. intelligence community off guard, which was the trip by North Korean leader Kim Jong-un to Beijing, where he met with Xi Jinping. The media are trying to say this is an outflanking of Trump, and it's a way the Chinese are flexing their muscles, but in fact, Trump's tweets seem to be very supportive of the visit. So what are your thoughts about this flanking action?

Zepp-LaRouche: This is certainly the overarching event of this past week. The ridiculous nature of the Western mainstream media is quite out in the open with news reports characterizing this North Korean-Chinese

heads-of-state meeting as "these two dictators meeting." This meeting is, in fact very, very good. Both Xi Jinping and Kim Jong-un discussed the long friendship between the two countries, North Korea and China. Kim Jong-un, in particular, promised to carry on policy in the tradition of his father and his family in the past. He said that he wants to work towards the denuclearization of the Korean Peninsula if the negotiations continue in an atmosphere of peace and with a constructive attitude. North Korea will, of course, need security guarantees; without that, he probably will not give up nuclear weapons.

But the fact that he went to China, and will meet with South Korean President Moon Jae-in at the end of April, and then, in all likelihood, with President Trump in May, means that one of the most dangerous possible hotspots that could lead to World War III, could be peacefully resolved.

Many contacts we have in South Korea have been telling us that these negotiations have an economic dimension. China—according to these sources—is going to build ports in North Korea on the east coast and the west coast. The whole question of the extension of the Belt and Road Initiative, involving South Korea, North Korea, Russia, and China,— that is the framework for truly stable development of this region.

Trump immediately tweeted that he got a phone call from President Xi Jinping, who told him that the meeting went very well. President Trump reported that he is extremely optimistic and looking forward, but that unfortunately, the sanctions against North Korea will have to be maintained until the problem is resolved. He is, however, looking forward to this upcoming summit.

This is *really* good, and it shows that with the right back-channels and, in this case, with all nations affected involved—Trump, Xi Jinping, Putin, and also Abe from Japan—that with this kind of diplomacy and negotiation, there is no problem on this planet which cannot be solved by people of good will. Everybody should be very happy about this development.

Schlanger: Absolutely. In the same context, there have been discussions in the United States about tariffs against Chinese imports. This could become a significant problem. But at the same time, there's a lot of discussion going on, including between Presidents Trump and Xi. What do you make of this discussion around the tariff fight?

Zepp-LaRouche: There is a very interesting response from China. Prime Minister Li Keqiang made a proposal: He said, rather than reducing the trade deficit by imposing tariffs, which could result in a trade war in which there would be no winner,— the other way to resolve the trade deficit would be to increase the volume of trade. That could include joint ventures between the United States and China with third countries. That is the approach that we have been proposing for a very long time.

There was also an extremely productive approach being discussed on CGTN, the China Global Television Network, which suggested a dialogue between the United States and China about infrastructure. Chinese investors could invest in the development of infrastructure in the United States through a fund. This is a proposal which we have promoted over an extended period: China has very large reserves of U.S. Treasury bonds, which don't do anything good, just sitting there. If those U.S. Treasuries were to be invested in U.S. infrastructure, through an infrastructure bank or some other mechanism, it would help to solve the financing problem which President Trump clearly faces.

What is presently available in terms of funding, is very far from the $1 trillion he talked about during the election campaign. The American Society of Civil En-

Xinhua/Ju Peng

North Korean leader Kim Jong Un (left) meeting with Chinese President Xi Jinping, in China, March 2018.

gineers reports that the actual requirement is not $1 trillion but $4.5 trillion. Other experts have said, in order to get modern infrastructure in the United States, you need $8 trillion in investment.

The trade imbalance could be eliminated by using Chinese expertise in high-speed train systems and other infrastructure. We in the Schiller Institute have developed and promoted this idea, to do in the United States what China has been doing and will complete by 2025, or perhaps 2020, to connect all its major cities through high-speed train systems. The infrastructure in the United States is in terrible shape and needs urgent repair; most of it is about 100 years old or even older. This is an approach to resolve the problem on a higher level.

People need to discuss this higher approach. There are many figures in the United States who have opened channels with their Chinese counterparts—the governor of West Virginia, the mayor of Houston, Texas, the governor of Alaska. Many people in Iowa are very tuned in, because former Iowa governor Terry Branstad is currently U.S. Ambassador in Beijing. There are alternatives to trade war, from which no one benefits.

Schlanger: I'd like more of your thoughts on this particular question. There is an effort to portray the idea of Chinese involvement in the United States as something Americans should be afraid of, should be wary of. And yet, as you point out, Alaska is working with China, also West Virginia. I think the mayor of Miami

was just in China. The mayor of Houston took a trade delegation there. This is part of a win-win policy. So, is there any reason Americans should be fearful that the Chinese have some devious, secret communist plot, to move in and take over the United States, by helping to rebuild the infrastructure there?

Zepp-LaRouche: People should ask themselves, where does this propaganda come from? It comes from neo-con think tanks, such as the CSIS and CFR in the United States, the European Council on Foreign Relations, and the Mercator Institute for China Studies (MERICS) in Germany. It comes from think tanks that are part of the British-dominated geopolitical faction, which is behind this confrontation against Russia and China, which we talked about earlier in this broadcast.

I strongly urge people to take a serious look at what China has been doing: Domestically, there is no country in the world which has so transformed itself as has China. I was in China for the first time in 1971, in the middle of the Cultural Revolution. At that time the country was completely distraught: people were unhappy and fearful. It was not a good period of Chinese history.

Since the reforms of Deng Xiaoping, and especially in the last five years of the Presidency of Xi Jinping,— China, in the last 40 years, has undergone a transformation which is without parallel. Seven-hundred million people have been lifted out of poverty. People are optimistic. The real root of Chinese culture is, for the last 2,500 years, Confucianism, which underlies the attitude today that there is no need to export the Chinese model. Unlike Christianity, which demands that all Christians should proselytize, should persuade other people to also become Christians, the Chinese have no such inclination. Confucianism is a philosophy which, to the contrary, is based on the idea of harmonious development.

Xi Jinping has emphasized, in every writing, in every speech, that this new "shared community for a common future of mankind" is based on total respect for the sovereignty of other countries, total respect for other countries' social systems, and that there is no intention to impose the Chinese model on any other country. China has offered to help developing countries overcome underdevelopment. This is win-win cooperation: That's the reason why 140 countries are now part of the New Silk Road. Win-win cooperation is in the interest of China, a very big country with a large population and 5,000 years of very rich cultural traditions. China is one of the major countries in the world, perhaps even the most important one, given the size of its population.

But China has no interest in imposing "Chinese characteristics" on anybody else. This is quite different from the neo-cons and neo-liberals, who have a policy of regime change, color revolution, export of democracy, and what they call "human rights." People should not be prejudiced. Take a fresh look, read the speeches of Xi Jinping, yourself. There is now a second volume out of *The Governance of China* by Xi Jinping, which is quite instructive. Look at other things, form your own opinion. I think you will see that the world has reached a point at which we *have* to overcome geopolitics.

If, at this point, the United States, or the West in general falls into the Thucydides Trap, taking the rise of China as a reason to move towards war and confrontation, it could very easily be the end of all humanity. We have to find a different way. China has said many times, it does not want to surpass the United States and replace it with a new unipolar world order, but that it wants a new alliance of sovereign countries with the idea of the oneness of humanity as a first principle.

This is a new concept of foreign policy; people should study it and relate to it, rather than blindly ac-

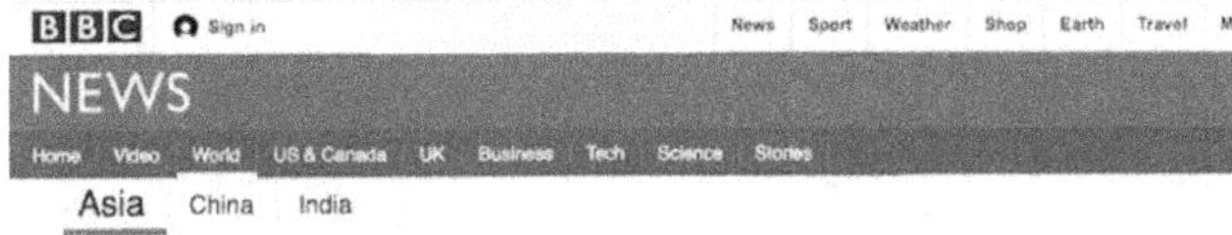

China accuses US of 'Cold War mentality' over nuclear policy

cepting the rather uninformed opinions of people like U.S. Senator Marco Rubio, who is on a rampage against anything Chinese. That rampage is not going to work. The rest of the world is very happy with what China is doing, which can work to the benefit of humanity if the United States and China find a way to cooperate in their mutual interest.

Schlanger: It's also significant that the people who are pushing this anti-China and anti-Russia line, and going toward a geopolitical conflict, are the same ones who are now the target of some of the new investigations, as the Mueller investigation continues to fall apart. The connection of MI6 agent Christopher Steele with the Skripal affair and the role of the Obama intelligence chiefs—Comey, Clapper, and Brennan—are coming up in the Congress. The Justice Department's Inspector General has just opened a new investigation.

Do you think, Helga, that it is possible that this will turn on them? Could this bring not only an end to the attacks on the President, but also an end to the reign of the geopoliticians over U.S. policy?

Zepp-LaRouche: The possibility is clearly there. The battle is not yet decided. The British empire—what we call the British empire—is not identical with the British government or the British people. When we say "British empire," we mean this system of leading financial institutions, investment banks, hedge funds, insurance companies, and multinational corporations, which are all interconnected with the private security apparatus. This is the neo-liberal model, which has ruled the world for the last several decades. These are the institutions that want to keep that system going. Many people are warning, correctly, that there is about to be another financial crash; remember, nothing has been done to eliminate the root causes of the 2008 crisis. This war provocation by Theresa May has everything to do with the fact that the transatlantic financial system is about to blow out.

Our listeners should not be complacent. This is not simply a legislative question, this is a political question and it's a systemic question. Fortunately, human nature is such that great evil can evoke an even greater good. My inclination is to be optimistic about the outcome of this battle. Given the role of the British in this provocation, and the role of the British empire in the coup against Trump, it is a very serious matter that requires a resolution.

One can only hope that the people of United States will mobilize themselves sufficiently to make sure that this investigation in Congress goes in the right direction. One can hope that Trump gets sufficient backup from his base of support, so that the efforts to derail his policies—whenever he has the impulse to have a good relationship with Russia, or with China for that matter—are not successful, and that his efforts *are* successful.

I call on all of you to become active. Don't sit on the sidelines as bystanders. Become active with the Schiller Institute. Help us spread the idea of this new alternative, the New Silk Road. We have to move humanity into a completely new era, where we, the many different peoples in this world, find a better way to work together. That is the real task. I invite you: Join the Schiller Institute, get in contact with us, help us to spread this message, and that way, you can do something to move humanity forward.

Schlanger: Well, Helga, there's so much happening; I want to make sure that we're not missing something. Is there anything else you want to bring up today?

Zepp-LaRouche: No. I think that is really what I wanted to say.

Schlanger: OK, well, very good! So, Happy Easter to you and to the viewers, and we'll be back next week.

hz.zepp@schiller-institut.de

Portugal Again Becomes A Hub of the Maritime Silk Road

by William Jones

April 1—The first Westerners to venture out to find a sea route to the East, after the land route had been closed by the conquest of the Middle East by the Ottoman Turks, were the Portuguese traders. The Portuguese explorer Vasco da Gama was the first European to sail around the southern tip of Africa and by that route reach India and lands further to the East. Da Gama was born in the port town of Sines, 166 km south of Lisbon. Sines is the largest deep water port in Portugal, and it is perhaps by a certain historical irony that da Gama's birthplace is on the verge of becoming one of the European hubs of China's enormous Belt and Road Initiative (BRI).

cc/APS

Port of Sines, Portugal.

The first missionaries to travel to China in the 16th Century were also from Portugal, and their first major port of call, which later became a Portuguese colony, was the island of Macau. Macau is today the most densely populated region in the world. While Han Chinese now make up 95% of its population, 2% is still of Portuguese and/or mixed Chinese/Portuguese descent, even after its return to China in 1999. Macau serves as an important transmission belt between China and the Portuguese-speaking countries in Europe, the Americas, and Africa. So the Portuguese connection to China is particularly strong, and when the BRI was launched by China's President Xi Jinping in 2013, the Portuguese in Macau—and in Lisbon—were following developments very closely.

In July 2016, China and Portugal signed a memorandum of cooperation which mentions Portugal's participation in the BRI. Portugal also confirmed that it was willing to issue debt on the Chinese financial market, becoming the first country in the Eurozone to issue so-called "Panda Bonds." Portuguese Prime Minister Antonio da Costa visited China in October 2016 and confirmed the country's interest in a close working relationship with China on the BRI.

In December 2016, some Portuguese businessmen and activists set up the New Silk Road Friends Association to help in lobbying to bringing the Belt and Road to Portugal. Fernanda Ilheu, the president of the association, said, I thought we needed a think-tank in Portugal for this initiative, to see how we can jointly build the

Portuguese Prime Minister Antonio da Costa.

Portugal's Minister of the Sea, Ana Paula Vitorino.

New Silk Road with China, mostly the Maritime Silk Road, where we have a lot of experience, tradition, and knowledge. Portugal needs to focus on this initiative, find out more, promote it, and understand how we can cooperate. That's the basis of our association."

Portugal in the World

Portugal is now working to have the new rail connections between Chongqing, China, and Madrid, Spain extended to Sines. There is already a tremendous amount of traffic, also coming through the 21st Century Maritime Silk Road, from Asia and Africa. Were Sines to be linked up with Madrid, this link would become a focal point for both of these Belt and the Road connections. This was discussed at a conference in Lisbon last month on the subject of Portugal's participation in the Belt and Road. The Chinese Ambassador to Portugal, Cai Run, who spoke there, said, "China values Portugal's role in the Belt and Road Initiative very highly and is willing to proactively push ahead with increased, pragmatic Chinese and Portuguese cooperation under the BRI framework." Hailing the initiative as "a great platform to promote mutual benefits" and "a new driving force for global economic growth," the ambassador described Portugal as "an important spot on the Maritime Silk Road."

The Port of Sines is also the first and largest artificial port of Portugal. It is surrounded by relatively calm waters. It is now working at capacity almost 24 hours a day. There are already plans for expanding the Sines port, and building another, even larger port, further north along the coast. Much of Chinese trade with Africa and with Europe transits Sines. It is also an important hub for trade from the Americas, and for trade transiting the Panama Canal. This will only increase if the Chongqing-Madrid line is extended to Sines.

China is also collaborating closely with Portugal on the development of aquatic technology, the so-called "blue economy." Portugal's Minister the Sea, Ana Paula Vitorino, accompanied by representatives of 39 Portuguese port and related companies, visited China last November to concretize Portugal's participation in the Maritime Silk Road. No specific details were made public, but the Portuguese businesses represented are leading port operators, construction companies, logistics operators, naval boatyard repair works, and engineering, energy, fishing, and aquaculture transformation companies.

Vitorino also met with the President of the Development Bank of China. She reported that agreements had been reached between Portuguese and Chinese companies to form consortia that would compete for several of the planned investment projects. A statement issued by the Ministry of the Sea said, "The visit is part of the dissemination of the strategy to increase the competitiveness of ports which includes, among others, new large-scale private projects like the new Container Terminal of Sines, Terminal Vasco da Gama; the New Barreiro Multimodal Terminal; and the new terminal in the port of Leixoes [near Porto in the north of Portugal], which are fundamental to increasing the capacity of the national ports."

Container Terminal XXI at the Port of Sines.

The British Are Selling—But Americans Are No Longer Buying

by Rachel Brown

April 2—To say that the world is unified under the direction of the honorable British leadership, would be as big of a lie as London's claims of Russian involvement in the poisoning of Sergei Skripal. Not only is the world not unified under the banner of the latest anti-Russian accusations by British Prime Minister Theresa May, with half of all EU nations refusing to expel Russian diplomats without proof, and Japan similarly—but the United States itself is not unified in its adherence to the British-run war drive either. Yes, the Trump Administration has formally followed protocol by enforcing diplomatic expulsions,

EIRNS/Eli Santiago

LaRouche PAC organizing in New York City.

but this was done without any personal vigor on the President's part, and right in the middle of the Skripal affair, Trump made a personal phone call to Russian President Putin, in which he did not even mention Skripal, the expulsions, or anything related to them. The President has made it clear that he intends to stay the course in working to improve relations with both Russia and China.

At the same time, the LaRouche Political Action Committee, now in the midst of an intensive 2018 political organizing drive, is discovering that millions of American citizens are slipping the British net. In city after city, and in a broad array of political venues, LPAC organizers are finding numerous individuals who are

thinking, questioning and discussing both present political events as well as the new policies which are urgently needed for the nation. From Maine to California, there is a widespread rejection of the lies which appear daily in the news media. Many of these people know that the British are lying, and they know that the charges of "Trump-Russian collusion" are nothing short of an attempted coup.

Throughout the nation, LaRouche movement organizers have intersected many and varied independent channels of response that don't cohere with so-called "accepted beliefs." LaRouche activists, led by the flagship Congressional campaign of Kesha Rogers, have been engaged in an intensive national organizing drive,

Kesha Rogers, petitioning to be on the ballot in Houston, Texas.

including everything from organizing on the street, to intervening in public meetings, to organizing for government action in State Legislatures, to holding educational forums to advance the necessary concepts of LaRouche's economic platform. This has included a highly successful online class series, with over 500 registered participants, which is developing the necessary higher ideas to create an entirely new economic paradigm. Participants are assigned reading material and homework, and are provided with interaction and feedback from the teachers, making it fully interactive and thorough.

In Detroit, several town hall meetings were held which included musicians, religious leaders of various denominations, infrastructure engineers, laborers, and people from both the "left" and "right" of the political spectrum. What unified the intention of the audience, during the question and answer sessions, was the optimism about the global economic renaissance, and the principle of the conscious creation of higher rates of productivity, via LaRouche's economic principles, as developed by LaRouche movement organizers.

In New York, organizers attended several pro-Trump political events, and were somewhat surprised to discover that these meetings were not only attended by the expected, profiled crowd.

People of all ethnic backgrounds were represented, and pro-Trump Obama supporters could even be found among the crowd at one Republican event. What unified all of these diverse people was the conviction that there is no Russian-Trump collusion, and that the FBI and DOJ are attempting a coup aimed at destroying the potential for improvement of the nation. Manhattan organizers also attended a youth rally in Brooklyn related to the Florida school shooting, and reported that many high school students were addressing issues much broader than gun laws. Almost none of those particular public youth speeches were reported by the media, yet they were delivered—and that alone signals that many of these youth want more than just the media-dictated script.

LaRouche organizers held a town hall meeting in the Baltimore area, where the subject of the financing of infrastructure was developed, as taken from the precedents of Abraham Lincoln and Franklin Roosevelt in the American System tradition. One federal level engineer stated that the American Society of Civil Engineers (ASCE) had been doing everything they could to illustrate the need for action, including

The campaign of Ron Wieczorek, Independent for Congress in South Dakota.

LaRouche PAC organizing in Greenwich, Conn.

by repeatedly giving U.S. infrastructure a 'D' grade report card, yet still nothing had been done. "Doesn't anyone in Washington understand what was going on?", he asked. LaRouche representative Paul Gallagher soberly noted that no, nobody does, and that is why the LaRouche movement's work is so essential. It is ironic that even experts at the federal level recognize that there must be a fundamental change in approach to the nation's basic needs, but they simply can't conceptualize the broader, underlying cultural problem.

Seattle organizers participated in a highly-attended forum on the Yemen war, and reported that besides the Congressman on the panel, other activist speakers were not unified on the CNN media line in their reporting. One D.C.-based activist emphasized that the Yemen war was begun under Obama, as emblematic of the foreign policy coming from both Presidents Bush and Obama, while other speakers explicitly stated that the United States is more to blame for the crimes in Yemen than is Saudi Arabia. After LaRouche organizers intervened with questions and statements about the potential of the New Silk Road for ending the Middle East wars, panelists agreed with them, and contributed their own thoughts on the need to end the fraudulent idea of a "uni-polar" world.

LaRouche activists also intervened in St. Paul, Minnesota public events, at a county Republican meeting in Texas, at public events and a youth march in Boston, and at a pro-Trump rally in the Washington, D.C. area led by a "Gays for Trump" activist. At all of these events they oriented the discussion towards the paradigm shift which can only be achieved by adopting LaRouche's Four Laws and joining the New Silk Road win-win new global paradigm.

There is a change going on in America. Increasingly, people are no longer buying the media pablum, and they are beginning to think for themselves. This is not "griping," nor is it populist rage. It is people talking to each other and looking for solutions. This is where the role of LaRouche PAC is indispensable.

For the last 50 years, millions of people have heard Lyndon LaRouche warning that the U.S. had been played the fool by the British. Many of these people are now looking at the despicable lies and warmongering from London, and reflecting back on who it was that was telling them the truth for all these years. They voted for Trump to end the wars, and they meant it. Despite massive lies and non-stop propaganda in the news media, millions of Americans are slipping out from under British control, and the imperialists are freaking out. It is clear that the "spirit of '76," though probably not explicitly recognized by most Americans, still exists, and it would be a mistake to underestimate the magnitude of American resistance to British imperial policies. The British are still selling their lies, but this time, Americans are not buying.

III. U.S. Idea More Mature than Europe

September 1, 2008

WHAT'S WRONG IN EUROPE?

Are You Neotenous?

by Lyndon H. LaRouche, Jr.

Not all genuinely evil people are also stupid. Take the case of Julian Huxley, who represented a social set which included the following: his grandfather Thomas Huxley; his own mentor and Satanist Aleister Crowley; H.G. Wells; Brigadier John Rawlings Rees; Bertrand Russell; and, Julian's brother Aldous. That collection was just about as evil as the British establishment types come. Nonetheless, Julian either came up with, or merely adopted a concept named "neoteny." He referred to a special case in which the species of a lower form of life stops its process of metamorphosis into adulthood, as at the larval phase, never enters the normal adult form of its species, and reproduces that larval, or comparable phase, in a sexually potent, "neo-adult" larval state. Imagine something like that being done, on a mass scale, to human beings; not in the customary sense of biological; but, culturally. As the clinical case of the 1968ers' "Weathermen" illustrates the case, it has been done to many among the Americans as it was to the European oligarchy.

Foreword: The Coming of the Larva

As you shall see when your study of this report has been completed, that it is significant that, since the assassination of President John F. Kennedy, only three Democratic Party nominees for President of the U.S.A. have been elected, since the President Lyndon B. Johnson, elected in 1964, who sensed the guns which sought to kill President de Gaulle, and had killed President Kennedy, as virtually aimed at the nape of his own neck. The two later cases were President Jimmy Carter, in 1976, and President Bill Clinton, the latter the last decent choice of actually incumbent President we have enjoyed, elected for two successive terms, in 1992 and 1996, respectively.

Notably, the two Bush-league Republican candidates elected since President Ronald Reagan's two terms, have turned out to have been shameful choices, or worse. President George H.W. Bush, had proven himself to have been a strategic and economic catastrophe, and his pathetic son, ostensibly chosen by George Shultz, and largely controlled in office by London-oriented Vice-President Dick Cheney, who has been something so low in character as beyond description in terms fit for the proverbial "ears of gentle ladies."

Now, in the coming election, we are presented with a choice between what presently appears to be two catastrophically incompetent nominees.

What I have just summarized, is a pattern which has prevailed, over most of what is approaching three generations since the death of President Franklin Roosevelt. Yet, no one should attempt to isolate the blame to any among those Presidents, as individuals, for this pattern of onrushing catastrophes. Something has gone wrong, not just with our political institutions, but with the decaying culture which has come to dominate the environment of the great majority of the U.S. citizenry (and, notably, also, a probably worse condition in west-

The Rolling Stones, aging emblems of the Baby-Boomer generation. Here, they are customizing their "signature" Mercedes-Benz, which cruised along with them on their "A Bigger Bang" concert tour (2005-07). The tour was done in partnership with Mercedes-Benz USA. (What's happened to the auto industry? Read on!)

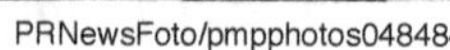

PRNewsFoto/pmpphotos048484

ern and central Europe as well). Our failed Presidents have been less the cause of our affliction, than a reflection of the culture which selected them as choices for that office. After all, who elected them? We are presently in the grip of a true, Classical tragedy, a virtually global catastrophe.

As you shall also see, hopefully, when this report is completed, that all this has much importance for those who wish to understand the why of what has happened to bring about the vanishing of our once actually U.S.-owned automobile industry.

As I have indicated in earlier reports, there have been three phases to the post-World War II process which has now landed us at the terminal end of that process of subversion and related corruptions which has now brought the world at large to the brink of a threatened planetary new dark age of mankind. First, there was the cultural shift downward, relative to President Franklin Roosevelt's time, under President Harry Truman. Second, there was the transition period from the assassination of President John F. Kennedy, to the turn of Spring 1968. Third, there has been the downward slide into physical-economic and cultural ruin which has been ongoing since the qualitative shift into a general physical-economic contraction, of 1968-1971.

The near dissolution of our U.S.-flag auto manufac-

turing industry, our keystone subject here, has been one of the notably crucial results.

The evidence of the rotting trend, not merely in selection of Presidents, but in the rotting quality of our own national culture over this interval, exposes a flaw in the pattern of design of our recent governments, a design which now echoes the commonplace "free trade" and kindred parliamentary traditions in a decadent Europe. This trend is presently overwhelming us. We can now virtually smell the threatened onset, like the sense of a great Summer storm, of a planetary New Dark Age, nearly everywhere in the U.S.A., today.

Thus, since the death of President Franklin Roosevelt, there has been a general trend, downward, among the top layers of the political life of our republic, especially since the assassination of President Kennedy. Even a decent President, or two, or three, within that interval, has not been sufficient, thus far, to reverse this trend in the overall state of the economy. However, now, it has turned much worse. Since the entry of the first George Bush administration, the U.S.A., as well as the governments of western and central Europe, have been plunged deeply into what is presently on the cliff's edge of becoming a global new dark age.

Since early February 2006, the U.S. Congressional

leadership under predatory Felix Rohatyn's and George Soros' virtually fascist control over Speaker of the House Nancy Pelosi, has become almost as bad in its performance as the Bush administration itself, and in its effects on current and coming events, worse.

We now see, thus, a pattern which suggests that we are on the verge of a perpetual descent into what threatens to become a permanently pathetic quality of government, a quality of change which suggests Julian Huxley's image of *neoteny*. We, with our so-called "Baby Boomers," are becoming, like western and central Europe, virtually a "living theater" performance of the *neotenous **The Lord of the Flies***.

Nonetheless, bad as things have become on both sides of the Atlantic, the past or present, self-inflicted tragedies of leading human cultures, were never inevitable. I am most probably the most successful economic forecaster over a period of more than four decades, but this is because, for scientific reasons, I never *predict* a crucial outcome, but only *forecast* the probable threat of an oncoming condition, and propose the actions which must be adopted if the threat of a fresh catastrophe is to be averted.

We must finally learn, contrary to those "kiss-breeches" and "suckfists" called our accountants and statisticians in general, that it is not "inevitable" trends which doom nations and their cultures, but, as the study of the history of tragedy shows, on and off the Classical stage, the typical root of afflictions such as our republic's own today, has been the present moment's lack of a popular acceptance of a good choice of leadership, if it were otherwise available, a leadership which might be qualified to chart a way out of ruin, which thus becomes a movement to safety. Where human creativity is suppressed, as in the decadence of leading universities and popular culture of recent decades, entropy moves in, as, most notably, since late Spring 1968.

Therefore, I have never "predicted;" as only bean-counters such as statisticians, and kindred fools have accused me of predicting. I do not predict; I propose a qualitative change from current directions, to escape what *otherwise* might be inevitable. In this matter, I have never erred in any long-range forecast, since my first, 1956, relatively short-term forecast of the great recession of 1957, as to occur about February-March 1957, and as I was the only known forecaster of what became the 1971 breakup of the Bretton Woods

The axolotl, a kind of salamander indigenous to Mexico, is neotenous all its life. Is this a trait shared by Presidents Bush 41 and 43? Let the reader judge. But for sure, both Presidencies have been a strategic and economic catastrophe.

system during the 1967-1971 interval The way out of today's Buppie-and-Boomer-led plunge into *neoteny,* is possible; but, only if we choose to bring on that possibility, instead of letting the alternative come by default.

On that account, as I shall stress, in appropriate moments in this report, Cardinal Nicholas of Cusa, who was otherwise one among the greatest builders of the best of modern history, is a key to defining the required quality of leadership needed for today.

1. Our Atlantic Era

The later, successful birth of modern European civilization as the successor to Europe's Fourteenth-Century New Dark Age, owed much to the devotion of Jeanne d'Arc, despite her martyrdom at English Norman hands. Contrary to the frauds by later British literary scoundrels treating that subject, the relevant drama of the great Friedrich Schiller followed faithfully the actually principled features of her case. The evidence is then clear, that her devotion in real life, inspired leaders of the Christian Church of that time, and led, by way of the great ecumenical Council of Florence, to the realization of the first modern European nation-state under France's great King Louis XI, a king much admired and copied by England's Henry VII, but, not Henry VIII, and not under the reign, to present date, of the British monarchy established under King George I.

However, we do have available options for saving civilization, if we are wise enough, and also able to secure the authority to choose them.

As I have said, repeatedly, on appropriate occasions, the crucial historical figure of that century has turned out to have been Cardinal Nicholas of Cusa, whose heritage has had three outstanding political features. First, the design for the establishment of the modern sovereign nation-state, his *Concordancia Catholica*. Second, his founding of all competent strains of modern physical science, his *De Docta Ignorantia*. Third, as I emphasize for the purpose of this occasion, is his posthumous inspiration of the Christopher Columbus who based himself on the counsel of Cusa in adopting his own devotion to crossing the Atlantic Ocean, a mission which Columbus adopted for the specific purpose which Cusa had specified in the writings which inspired Columbus to this end.

The case which I have thus set before you now, has been properly introduced in those terms of reference.

The New World

In the case of the inspiration for the founding of the English-speaking colonies in North America, the lead-ing colonists and their backers followed a precedent implicit in what are termed in modern times as ancient, Classical, so-called Greek sources. That ancient culture was, notably, a principal maritime culture of the Mediterranean, which referenced the existence of a still earlier, Atlantic maritime culture. It was, so to speak, in the bones of that far-ranging maritime tradition, that the apparent futility of living in a certain habitual place which was then deemed to represent incurable cultural faults, would impel bold souls to organize a flotilla for movement to a new colony deemed to represent a quality of advantage, such as that of a relatively safe distance from their present, culturally contaminated habitation.

The outcome of the practice of that lesson from Classical Greece, had included, prominently, Cusa's recommendation for escaping the depraved situation in the Mediterranean region after the fall of Constantinople. Cusa's specifications, with included, relevant scientific-technical details supplied by Cusa's circles, were what prompted Columbus, from about A.D. 1480 on, to make the later, 1492 and later trans-Atlantic passages to the continent on the opposite shore. The first passages required approximately the lapse of time which Columbus expected.

This passage inspired the wave of trans-Atlantic colonization, by proffering, as Sir Thomas More's *Utopia* implied, the opportunity to colonize a new place at a relatively safe distance from the cultural depravity which reigned under the then-existing Venetian and associated oligarchy within Europe, an infestation of neo-Venetian oligarchism which prevails in Europe, still, today, in the underlying intention of the parliamentary and related oligarchical relics of so-called "feudalism" there today.

The success of the American Revolution, actually over the period 1763-1789, following the British decision to crush the English colonies in North America, reflected an earlier decision made in the context of the February 1763 Treaty of Paris. That decision provoked the colonists into forming what thus became the leading realization of the intention of that colonization which had been set into motion earlier by the influence of Nicholas of Cusa on the intentions of navigator Christopher Columbus.

This notion of the benefit to mankind of colonization in distant lands, has been the root of the functional significance of the American English-speaking colonies in North America, to the present day. This is also what General Douglas MacArthur recognized in Curtin's Australia. That has been the potential which U.S. leaders such as John Quincy Adams, in crafting President Monroe's "doctrine," recognized in the future of the formation of the independent, post-colonial, sovereign states of Central and South America, once those states were freed from control by Europe's Anglo-Dutch Liberal tyranny. This is the underlying, long-ranging, crucial importance of the United States, even as debased as it has become, to the present day.

That then, already existing problem of Europe which Cusa recognized in his time, persists to the present day. The potential remedy is now also expressed in the special importance, for humanity at large, of the development of the great Asian nations, such as China and India today. This is the source of the continued special significance of Russia today, as being, not merely Russia's vast resources, but its historic mission as the world's leading *Eurasian* culture, a culture upon whose revived, U.S-modeled, science-driven industrial development in the tradition of Franklin Roosevelt, much of the possibility of a happy future for western and central Europe now depends.

Since Cusa, France's Louis XI, and England's Henry VII, there have been some relatively great periods in this or that nook of modern European culture. Post-Westphalia France under the influence of Cardinal Mazarin and Jean-Baptiste Colbert, is an outstanding case, as was a brief period of Queen Anne's England under the influence of Gottfried Leibniz, and the mid-to-late Eighteenth-Century, Classical movement under the leadership of such as Abraham Kästner, Gotthold Lessing and Moses Mendelssohn, and under Josef Haydn, Wolfgang Mozart, Lazare Carnot, Goethe, Friedrich Schiller, and the Humboldt brothers, and under the leadership of the Carl F. Gauss, Lejeune Dirichlet, and Bernhard Riemann of the 1840s and 1850s. There was a later kind of Renaissance in

Christopher Columbus's trans-Atlantic passages were prompted by the scientific work of Nicholas of Cusa and his circles. Later came "a flood of Europeans migrating from corrupted Europe into new settlements such as those of pre-1689 Massachusetts."

Europe, following, and largely shaped by the U.S. victory over the British Empire and its Confederacy puppet over a period during the 1860s, into the 1880s, until the ouster of Bismarck in 1890.[1]

The Sickness

Yet, in all, as we in the U.S.A., and the Americas generally, have felt the ebbs and flows of the cultural tides of civilization in Europe, for worse or better, not only during the Eighteenth Century, but over the course of the span of the rise of the U.S. to become a great power during the Nineteenth Century as a whole, the oligarchical weaknesses in "Old Europe" have been the source, time and time again, for us and for other nations, of the same worst afflictions, such as the types of Rohatyn and Soros, transported to us, here.

Largely as a result of the two so-called "world wars" created by the London-centered Anglo-Dutch Liberal interests, Europe still carries the endemic moral sick-

---

1. It is necessary to point out one error in Germany's policy which haunts Germany still to the present day. The action by Prussia against the attack from France under Britain's puppet, Napoleon III, was correct; but, the desire by Prussia to continue that war after the abdication of Napoleon III, had tragic consequences which were evident to some even at that time. By failing to offer France an honorable peace at the point of Napoleon's abdication, Wilhelm I's monarchy sealed the potential for what became France's future role, later, as a hardened asset of Britain after the twin effects of the assassination of President Sadi Carnot and the Dreyfus affair. The "First World War" launched by Britain was made possible by this piece of folly, and, similarly, the "Second." This continued until President Charles de Gaulle's "Europe from the Atlantic to the Urals" alliance with Germany's Chancellor Konrad Adenauer, an anti-British action by de Gaulle, to which London responded by pushing the massive efforts at assassination of de Gaulle by his London-centered array of adversaries, which also led to the direct role of London in pushing the early resignation of Adenauer in favor of the German Liberal faction in Adenauer's own party. The rape of Germany by London (and Britain's anti-de Gaulle asset, Mitterrand) after 1989, must, therefore, be recognized as a continuing effect of the role which Britain has assigned to France, a British policy which is to be seen as a continuation of London's role in orchestrating that Seven Years War, by means of which the British East India Company became an imperial power.

ness from which the leading colonists of North America fled, a legacy of the neo-medieval oligarchism of parliamentary systems, from which our leading colonists had fled, but of which Europe has yet to be cured. This has been a sickness which arrives in the Americas, again and again, like flotsam, as if with the new dawn's coming upon our Atlantic shore, a disease known as the Anglo-Dutch Liberalism which, among other flotsam, gave the world Mussolini and Hitler. It is a financier-oligarchical sickness, which could prove fatal, unless cured very soon, or, otherwise, the United States, too, will go down to a virtual Hell born of the spread of imported financier-oligarchical tyrannies typified by the predatory, alien grip of foreign financier predators on the U.S.A. today.

What has made possible this presently recent, moral degeneration of our own U.S. political system, a descent into its advanced state of decadent, political and economic morbidity since the mid-1960s, today, is a fungus typified by the rise of what became an artificially shaped, *neotenous* generation developed in that pathological form, from among the suburban layer born into the "White Collar" and "Organization Man" breed, between 1945 and about 1958.

This *neotenous* degeneration emerged in the U.S. of the middle to late 1960s, as a specific part of a larger generation aptly compared to the youth of the children and adolescents of the ostensibly fictional ***The Lord of the Flies.*** Today, this social formation, represented chiefly in a certain part of the generation now in their fifties and sixties, has distinguishing characteristics, as a kind of special caste-formation, which is anti-"blue-collar," anti-farmer, anti-nuclear, and neo-malthusianist, as this is merely typified by the co-thinkers of an obnoxious royal London pet from Possum Hollow, former U.S. Vice-President Al Gore.

The same pathological influence developed in the relevant "white collar" households of that time, was replicated in Europe in a particularly vicious form of intellectual and moral degeneration, under the influence of an existentialist, implicitly pro-Satanic, Congress for Cultural Freedom and, in a related form, the influence of such as Crowley, H.G. Wells, Bertrand Russell, and the Cambridge Systems Analysis group, an influence spread into the Soviet Union in such Russell outgrowths as the Laxenberg, Austria International Institute for Applied Systems Analysis (IIASA).

That aspect of "the Baby Boomer" culture, as reflected back within the U.S.A. itself, typifies the notion of a *neotenous* form of human cultural degeneration in the modern world of European culture today.

This is what has happened to ruin many of the people of the United States culturally and morally: most notably among the Baby-Boomer caste-formation. We should recognize an earlier, even ancient precedent for this in a similar, Dionysian, or Dionysian-like pattern in the decline of many modern, medieval, and ancient cultures. We should recognize it in perspective when we contrast such types of Baby-Boomers and their culturally specific forms of conditioning by the "White Collar" and "Organization Man" cults of the 1950s, with what we should have recognized as the genius expressed in the design of the ancient great pyramid of Giza, or in the related case of the acquisition of knowledge of the form of physical science known as *Sphaerics* by such as the Pythagoreans and Plato.

The relevant evidence of this, is that, often, in history or credible evidence of pre-history from deep into the last great wave of glaciation, many known cultures have been progressive offshoots of a reaction against the degeneration of earlier ones: just as the constitutional system founded by immigrants to the colonization of the Americas was expressed in the establishment of the United States, as an escape from the persisting decadence within "Old Europe."

We also have some clinically conclusive evidence of the way in which the reverse of such cultural degeneration occurs. Usually, some part of society moves away from the degenerated part of its current culture, usually by basing its fresh development on nurturing evidence from an earlier cultural renaissance. Just so, the rebirth of ancient physical science, in the form of the modern European science, was built on the foundations of such as the Pythagoreans and Plato, and the program of colonization, defined by Cardinal Nicholas of Cusa, which sent Christopher Columbus across the Atlantic to lead a flood of Europeans migrating from corrupted Europe into new settlements such as those of pre-1689 Massachusetts.

We do not know presently, how many times in the existence of the human species, that a renaissance has expressed the legacy of an earlier, relatively superior form of culture. The best evidence of a categorical quality known for this purpose, is the evidence of the roots of competent physical scientific practice in the development of astronomy by ancient, transoceanic maritime cultures existing during the long glaciation of a time when the ocean levels were about as much as four hundred feet below current ones.

We also know, that the great change in economy and statecraft which has shaped the course of world events since the U.S. victory over London's Confederacy puppet, was, most emphatically, the effect of the development of the U.S. transcontinental railway system as the crucial shift in the nature of modern economy which has been the threat to which the British empire reacted with its preparation and launching of that change in world affairs typified by that empire's orchestration of launching the horrid events typified by both of two "world wars," the so-called "cold war," and the present effort to eradicate the institution of the sovereign nation-state through the proposed new "Tower of Babel" called "globalization.

We should have known, by now, that unless we defended the character of our United States as a refuge from the endemic sickness of Europe, that that creeping sickness would take us over, as we find the hand of British corruption of the minds and bodies of our institutions and of so many among our citizens controlling our nation's will and destiny now. "Globalization," expressed typically as so-called "environmentalism," is that potentially fatal, creeping sickness.

That is what is expressed in the form of the spreading "neoteny" spread by our Baby Boomers and their like today. Such is the present crisis of "The Atlantic Era," the crisis engulfing the world today.

2. The Coming of the Baby Boomers

As I have outlined the evidence in sundry earlier locations, the "Baby Boomers" and their echo in the phenomenon called the "Buppies," is a sickness, not a lawfully natural phenomenon of healthy human minds. Without the moral sickness which that section of the population represents, the present economic crisis of the United States, including, specifically, the destruction of the American-owned auto industry, could not have happened.

This matter requires a brief introduction into the relevant areas of deep background.

The "Baby Boomers" are not a generation, but, rather a "degeneration." They are not an age-group, even though they are, principally, part of an age-group. They are a social-economic *caste*.

We do, or could know a great deal about characteristics of "class," "caste," and other special behavior in some types of historically defined societies. All in all, the best insight into "naturally human behavior" of all cultural varieties of mankind, is available to us through studies of the ways such phenomena emerge in various expressions of cultural evolutions. What we can fairly say that we actually "know" about cultures, is what we are able to prove to be some of the ways in which the knowable principles of "naturally human behavior" are expressed, or suppressed in cultures which evidence permits us to examine more or less closely.

What we actually know about the matter of social *neoteny* considered in this present report, is clear evidence that most of what we tend to regard, especially academically, as principles of "sociology" or "cultural anthropology," or "law," is a well-defined topic if and when it is considered as the product of what should prove to have been some clearly definable sort of hocus-pocus, or, perhaps, simply the usual case of those apparently literate persons who mistake mere "information" (e.g., "facts") for human "intelligence." However, there is nothing properly called "natural" about the mode in which the massively "brainwashed" class of "Baby Boomers" in the 50-65 age-group today came into being.[2] It is not a "social class;" it is a "caste," which, in this case, is distinguished by the caste's cult-like trappings of something like a primitive religion with, like the famous de-composed Richard Wagner, specifically Dionysian-like characteristics.[3]

To understand that caste, and its effects on society, what we actually know about the principled nature of mankind in general, is the fact that there is probably no part of mankind as a whole which lacks the manifestly

---

2. E.g., "Buppies" and "Boomers."
3. Conductor Wilhelm Furtwängler was, unquestionably a genius, despite his defense of Wagner's work. Furtwängler's error on this account, was his affinity to the idea of a tradition of "German music," as distinct from the contrary notion of "German" by Hermann Göring's favorite oompah-bandmaster, Herbert von Karajan. Such are the pitfalls of the sometimes extraneous presumptions co-opted by a great mind.

"inborn" distinction of the human individual from all lower forms of life: *creativity*, as I use that term in matters of physical science and Classical artistic composition. Yet, the characteristic of most known societies is the systematic suppression of that creative potential among the largest part of a society's population. The pro-Malthusian and related characteristics of the phenomenon of the Baby-Boomer caste formation, are typical expressions of the characteristic of that social formation as a quasi-religious cult, a specifically Dionysian (e.g., pro-Satanic) caste.

Among English-Speakers

The typical root of this specific, "Baby Boomer" and kindred brutalization of intellectual life in the English-speaking world, is the phenomenon of so-called "Liberalism." Liberals in general are not necessarily "Baby Boomers;" rather, the Baby Boomers as a caste-formation, are a case of a fanatical cult-form, derived from the foundation of the specifically Ockhamite, as distinct from Aristotelean irrationalism. Sarpi's neo-Ockhamite system of what became modern Anglo-Dutch Liberalism, the social base of what was built up in what became, under Sarpi's influence, the maritime regions of what became his Protestant northern Europe. That term, Liberalism, strictly employed, signifies the substitution of induced customs as replacement for the functions of actual human intelligence, as in the case of the specifically Sarpian form of deluded belief induced among academics duped into genuflecting before the delusion that Isaac Newton was a scientist, or the similarly foolish idea that Euler made honest objections to Leibniz's concept of the infinitesimal.

What we know of the principles of human intelligence, is chiefly what we know of the way in which creativity is suppressed among, for example, the typical university graduate, and others, of our society today, as the point is made in the video production on the subject of the Baby-Boomer's hand in crafting the specific quality of decadence commonplace to the teaching of academic science today, "The Harvard Yard."[4] In this and related cases, *customary taught belief* is substituted for actual scientific proof, and the ritual of a virtually proprietary, descriptive language of mathematical formulations is substituted, as by Liberalism (e.g., empiricism, positivism), for actual

knowledge of experimentally validated natural principles.

In the U.S.A. today, for example, the typical standard of mental behavior in nearly all social classes, is the desire to be overheard saying what will be accepted among the members of the social grouping to which one's ego is appealing for recognition and affectionate stroking. Such people do not recognize their behavior for what it is: They are, in effect, being efficiently "brainwashed."

At the present moment, a sweeping shift in cultural trends is under way in the U.S.A., in particular. It is a shift of authority during the recent two years, even if it is only one in progress, a shift away from the largely self-discredited "68ers" of the political class most clearly, toward the potential new center of leading social influence in political life, a layer centered presently in their 40's. We in the U.S.A. are as if caught in political midstream, between the present hegemony of the domination of our political and related life by a caste-like formation within the generation in their fifties and sixties, who have lost their way, and, on the other hand, those only presently at the verge of establishing their leading influence. That has been most emphatically the experience of the recent Democratic Party Presidential primary campaigns.

In this transition, the worst of the lot still in leading positions are the traditionally "white collar" "sixty-eighter" expressions of a lunatic cult like that of the English Luddites of the early Nineteenth Century, today's artificially induced, mentally diseased cult of post-industrial "environmentalism," as typified, in a typically disgusting form, by the case of virtual American moral expatriate, Soros-related, former Vice-President Al Gore.

To illustrate the way in which a caste-formation (as distinct from a social class) operates inside the U.S.A. today, take the clinical case of the entirely arbitrary destruction of the U.S.A.'s own automobile industry by this "Baby-Boomer" cult.

The 'Auto Industry' Syndrome

The last gasp of the credibility of the "Baby Boomer" generation came, largely at my prompting, during the immediate aftermath of the November 2004 Presidential election. I called out to the Baby Boomer leadership in the ranks of the Democratic Party, and elsewhere, to get up off the floor of the dubiously certified defeat of the Kerry Presidential campaign, and rally to defend

---

4. See www.larouchepac.com.

Social Security against the lunatic efforts to loot and wreck it, efforts coming from the George W. Bush, Jr. Administration.

The Democratic Party stalwarts and also some key Republicans rallied to this patriotic cause—until February 2006.

In the meantime, at the close of 2004, I launched an effort to save the machine-tool-centered economic potential of the U.S. auto industry against evident clear intentions to shut down that last major bastion of what the U.S. economy had once been. In the Spring of 2005, the frankly fascist Felix Rohatyn of "Big Mac" and "Pinochet" notoriety, intervened directly against me, arguing that I was, in effect, a potential new "Franklin Roosevelt," and that this, and my role must be stopped. In February 2006, the Congressional leadership capitulated to Rohatyn's line, and the U.S. auto industry has virtually disappeared, and with it most of the once-great political-economic power of the U.S.A.

The U.S. Congress has been virtually dead under "Squeaker" of the House Nancy Pelosi, ever since February 2006. However Pelosi could not have conducted the wrecking job which she has done for the advantage of Rohatyn and George Soros, to date, but for the "Baby Boomer" factor inside the Congress and that Boomer age-group's leadership of the Democratic Party generally.

As I had emphasized from the close of 2004 onwards, it would be impossible to "save" the auto industry in its present form. The post-industrial orientation launched against the Franklin Roosevelt legacy after the close of World War II, had focused on using the automobile and related aircraft industries as a way of shutting down what had been the bulwark of the great U.S. industrial revolution since the mid-Nineteenth Century, the agro-industrial development based on the role of the emergence of a transcontinental railway system.

There are, in fact, two automobile industries. One is a manufacturing industry; the other is the worship of a cult of worship of the Boomer's modern golden calf, the car. In recent times, that manufacturing industry has virtually disappeared. Such a variety of industry exists, and has operating branches inside the U.S.A.; but, it is a foreign industry which has ceased to exist as an actual U.S. industry, like many other former U.S. industries which have either virtually died out, or are expressed for Americans, chiefly, in terms of products made by foreign interests, even when not by foreign sources.

3. The Myth of the Automobile

The development of transcontinental railway systems, had been a U.S.-piloted, modern supplement to Charlemagne's pioneering development of a European system of inland waterways. This development became the driver of the great agro-industrial development of the U.S.A. and its power in the world from President Lincoln's administration onward. The essential feature of this industrial revolution over the period from President Lincoln through President Franklin Roosevelt, had been *the build-up of the scientific potential represented by the machine-tool sector*, and the great development of the industries which developed knowledge and practice of scientific principles into the form of a highly developed machine-tool skill through whose role large-scale and other manufacturing industries, were established. Formerly, many among these industries had been world leaders. Since about Fiscal Year 1967-68, that U.S.A. economy has been gripped by a process of destruction by the complicity between its own government and ruling Anglo-American financier interests.

The history of the U.S. automobile industry since that time, has been closely tied with the British empire's fear, which it experienced during 1863-1865, a fear expressed in the view that the United States under President Abraham Lincoln was probably going to defeat London's puppet, the Confederacy, in the course of Lincoln's commitment to defending the Union. This turn in the course of that Civil War did not actually kill Lord Palmerston; but, it did ruin the policies of attempted containment, dissolution, and other systemic wrecking of the U.S.A. which the British Foreign Office of Lord Shelburne's Jeremy Bentham (and Bentham's successor Palmerston) had played since the closing years of the U.S. War of Independence until Lincoln's victory.

It was the development of the transcontinental railway system, especially as by the methods unleashed under President Lincoln, which had brought into being a quality of the U.S. republic as Secretary of State and President John Quincy Adams had intended, a republic which would become a transcontinental sovereign within its Atlantic, Pacific, Canadian, and Mexican borders.

This was a U.S. achievement which also became known as the "geopolitical" threat to the British maritime power represented by the effect of the industrial,

Library of Congress

Completion of the transcontinental railroad in 1869, joining the Union and Central Pacific lines at Promontory Summit, Utah. Although completed after President Lincoln's death, this was one of the crowning features of his Presidency, and his life-long work for "internal improvements."

agricultural, and railway development of the U.S.A., as this was manifest over the course of the 1861-1876 interval. This U.S. development was one of the leading reasons that the British assassinated Lincoln, and, probably were directly engaged, later, in the strategically crucial assassination of President McKinley, as well. This was the motive, and remains the motive of the London imperialists to the present moment.[5]

EIRNS/Stuart Lewis

The deconstruction of the U.S. railroads is in evidence across the nation; this picture was taken in Brunswick, Maryland, in 1987.

---

5. The actual authorship of what is called "9-11" is no longer efficiently concealed.

The U.S. Railroad Grid in 1870, After Completion of the Transcontinental Railroad

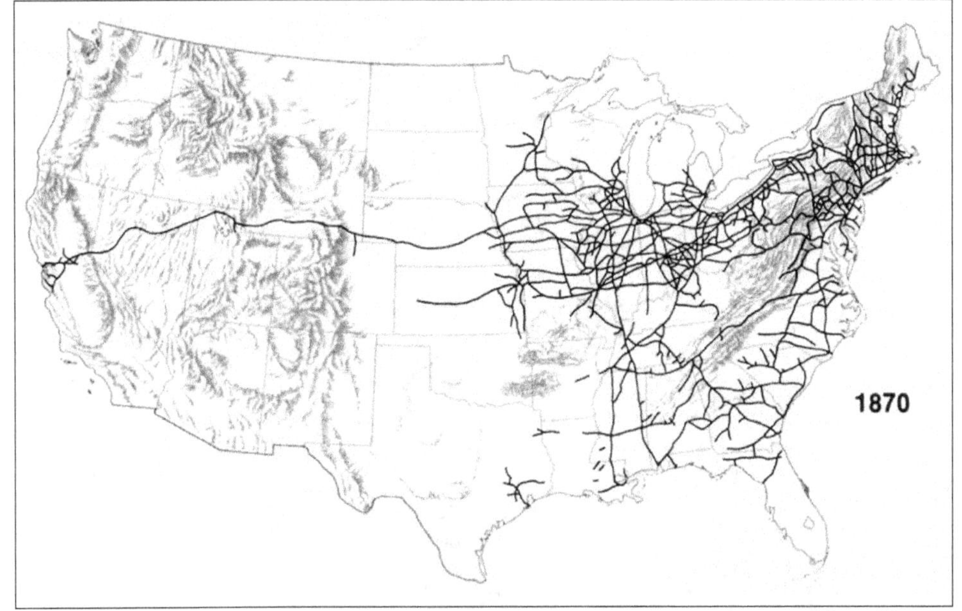

Library of Congress

In two World Wars, the influence of the U.S.A. on continental Eurasian development, and the vast superiority of American economic methods over those of the British Empire, signaled to London that the U.S.A. must be destroyed, if the British Empire were to continue to rule the waves of the world.

Any political, or military strategist who does not recognize this most essential feature of world history as a whole since 1863-1865, is virtually an idiot in the matter of strategic outlook on world affairs, however skilled he, or she might be in the relatively minor arts of the military and diplomatic trades.

The creation of the post-World War II "Baby Boomer" generation (were "de-generation" not a better term) is essentially a post-World War II, Truman Administration-promoted, but chiefly British-crafted outgrowth of this strategic reality of the essential, mortal conflict between the U.S.A. patriots and the British imperial design of its monetary system.[6] The way in which the automobile industry had been built up (most notably, since the 1920s), and the U.S. railway system taken down (actually beginning, about 1926, but, more emphatically, after the close of World War II), is a crucially revealing aspect of this existential form of strategic cultural conflict between the patriots of the U.S.A., and our republic's principal foes of the entire 1763-2008 interval to date, the British imperialists and their American assets within our economy and political parties.

The way in which the U.S. automobile industry was, undeniably, first, built up, to undermine the railway systems, and then taken down, as now, can not be competently assessed without taking into account such crucial issues as the strategic superiority of rail, and comparable mass-transit systems over personal automobiles as a mode for transport of people, or of high-value-density, or very heavy freight over medium to long distances.

This means, that while the automobile as a supplementary means of personal transportation, has a significant, continuing place in daily life, the replacement of mass transport systems by individually operated transport, has been, in large, an expression, at higher strategic levels, of a more or less fully witting intent to bring down the United States' economy, and, thus, the power of the United States otherwise.

No sane person could honestly deny that the combination of increased reliance on highway commuting by

---

6. During and following World War II, the U.S. intelligence community was divided, "essentially," between two factions, as typified by the case of two factions inside the Office of Strategic Services (OSS). The one, associated with OSS chief General Donovan ("Donovan's boys"), and the opposing "white shoe" gang centered in Ivy League, "Wall Street"- and London-oriented types, who emerged around the Dulles brothers.

Although I was never part of this then, I came to identify myself with the remains of the patriotic legacy of Donovan et al. at a later point in my life, not as a recruit, but as a meeting of the minds among patriots with converging experiences. This resulted in a virtual war within wars between the patriots and the "white shoe" types, with a third set occupying a middle-ground, still today. The Truman Presidency was a temporary victory of that "other side," closer, by instinct, to Churchill's London, than to the patriotic U.S. tradition.

trucks and passenger vehicles has ruined the standard of living of households who have been victimized by the increase of lapsed time in commuting. No sane person, and no competent accountant, could deny the importance of replacing that costly highway congestion by mass transit systems. No competent economist could deny that the need to replace lost railway transport by short-haul airline traffic has contributed to the ruin of many things, including the airlines and airport facilities.[7]

It should therefore be obvious, that any political figure who does not grasp, and concur with the point I have just made, is not competent to serve as President of the U.S.A. at this time.

Once such facts are recognized and understood, there is no real mystery about either the why or the how of the manner in which that aberrant caste-formation, the "Baby Boomers," was created synthetically inside the U.S.A. and in western Europe beginning the close of World War II. Taking the issues in the light of the alien role of the Baby-Boomer caste, consider the difference between an automobile as a useful tool for certain specific kinds of cases of transportation, and the use of the automobile as a virtually

Passenger Rail Grid Shrinks Drastically, 1967 to 2005

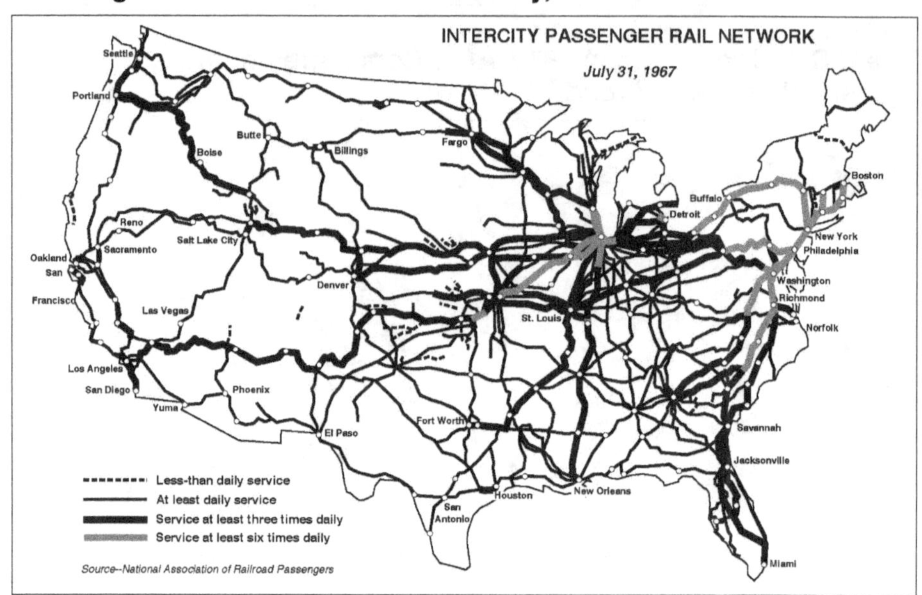

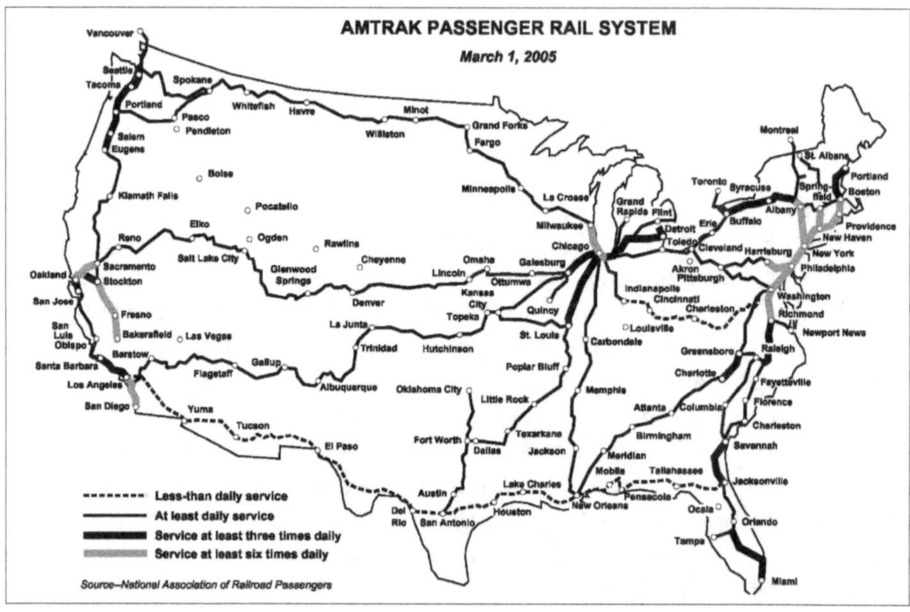

Nationwide passenger rail miles fell from 65,852 in 1967, to 21,807 in 2005, a 67% decrease. A map sequence of this decline is available at www.narprail.org. Animation-studies of this and other trends were published at www.larouchepub.com during 2005, and are archived at the site.

sexual expression of a cult-formation.[8]

Look at the most relevant expression of not only the obscene noises from the rumble-seat of the past, but today's proverbial, often rage-driven "nut behind the wheel," the Baby Boomer today.

---

7. With the development of magnetic-levitation replacements for friction-rail systems, we have not only touched ground speeds of 300 miles per hour, or greater, but have available methods of handling of freight classification without the accustomed jams of railway freight systems. Under these conditions, the door-to-door lapse of time for medium-haul not only competes with air transport, but is much cheaper in physically-determined costs. So, nuclear-power is inherently less costly, when properly developed and used, than any other mode of fueled system today.

8. There was a time when it could have been said, that, "It is no longer necessary to drive into the woods, or crawl into a rumble-seat, to make babies."

The Boomer as Your Enemy

The emergence of the Baby Boomer generation[9] from its egg-and-early-larval stages, during the late 1960s, and that generation's *neotenously* quasi-adult phase as "the 68ers,"[10] was the expression of the work of the circles of followers of Aleister Crowley, H.G. Wells, and Bertrand Russell of the 1920s and 1930s. Russell, in the post-World War II decades, emphasized his continuation of the Wells-Russell project which Russell identified publicly as his contribution to World Government established through Nuclear Warfare, beginning in his contribution to the September 1946 issue of the *Bulletin of the Atomic Scientists*.

The Bertrand Russell of the late 1940s and beyond, while lacking Wells' earthy ways, but equally nasty in other respects, was, essentially, echoing both H.G. Wells' *The Open Conspiracy* and *The Shape of Things to Come*.[11] By the end of the war, with Wells dead, Russell carried on through such channels as the later establishment of his penetration of the Soviet Union through his World Parliamentarians for World Government, and through the Club of Rome-linked, Laxenberg, Austria International Institute for Applied Systems Analysis (IIASA) as an outlet for the influence of Russell's Cambridge Systems Analysis cult's penetration of the Soviet system, and beyond.[12] This same crew played a crucial leading part, together with Britain's Prince Philip and his crony, *former SS official* Prince Bernhard of the Netherlands, and, thus, with Dame Margaret Mead, in the creating and continuing sponsoring of the Club of Rome and related associations such as the World Wildlife Fund.[13]

If you wish to ask, what was Russell's motive, read relevant excerpts taken from[14] Russell's *Prospects of Industrial Civilization*[15] and his later *The Impact of Science on Society*.[16]

From the former, read: "The decay of individual passions brings with it, first of all, a diminution of individuality. In a thoroughly industrialized community, such as the United States, there is little appreciable difference between one person and another;... A lunatic who kills his wife with every circumstance of horror, is a public benefactor, since he livens things up."

Then, from Russell's *Impact of Science on Society*, consider the revealing following excerpts:

"Bad times, you say, are exceptional, and can be dealt with by exceptional methods. This has been more or less true during the honeymoon period of industrialism, but it will not remain true unless the increase of population can be enormously diminished. At present [1953] the population of the world is increasing at about 58,000 per diem. War, so far, has had no very great

---

9. In essential respects, a generation which appeared, as a generation of "white collar" attributes, during the post-war interval 1945-1958, between the "book-ends" of V-E and V-J days, on the one side, and the relative depths of the 1957-58 recession, a generation which fits roughly, as a caste-formation, into the categories of two books from the 1950s, *White Collar* and *The Organization Man*, and from the influence of such devotees of the evil H.G. Wells and Bertrand Russell as Professor Norbert Wiener. and John von Neumann. The Anglo-American cult (e.g., the Congress for Cultural Freedom) of the systemic irrationalism of the Frankfurt School existentialism of Heidegger, Theodor Adorno, Hannah Arendt, and cult-writings such as *The Authoritarian Personality*, is among the notable markers of that trans-Atlantic cult-formation.

10. The use of the issues of the Vietnam War in lowering the voting age, is a correlative of the factor of neoteny (e.g., *The Lord of the Flies*) in the emergence of the Baby-Boomer caste.

11. The actual origin of the Fabian Society's influence in shaping the plans for World Wars I and II was the same H.G. Wells, trained under Julian Huxley's grandfather. Wells' *The Open Conspiracy* of 1928, and Russell's endorsement of its theses is notable; but it is with Wells' 1933 draft of the warfare-scenario of *The Shape of Things to Come* that the war issue is made clear. It is these schemes by the Fabian Wells and Russell which are the context of the intention which created the synthetic cult of the Baby-Boomer generation as a caste-formation now popularly referenced as "the 68ers." Beginning his invitation to Soviet General Secretary Nikita Khrushchev to participate in Russell's meeting of World Parliamentarians for World Government, Russell emerged as a chief architect of both the plans for thermonuclear confrontation with the Soviet Union and the breakup of the Soviet Union under Gorbachov.

12. The same Soviet and Euro-oligarchical circles associated with British penetration of the Soviet system by IIASA overlap those leading Soviet personnel who brought about British agent George Soros' penetration of Russia during the 1990s.

13. An embittered enemy of mine from Columbia University days, the late, and thoroughly evil Dame Margaret Mead, a former backer of Professor Norbert Wiener's RLE operations at MIT and kindred operations, was wielding what was quite literally her witch's staff, as she pursued my then-future wife, the still athletic Helga Zepp, with Mead's witch's staff through the premises of a 1974 conference on world population control at Bucharest, Romania. Helga pranced merrily in great amusement at the spectacle of Mead's efforts to appear monstrous without the means to actually reach a Helga who pranced always at a safe distance from the lurching hulk of Mead. Then German journalist Helga had challenged conference spokesman John D. Rockefeller III on the Nazi precedents for what he was promoting there. Mead who had once come in Samoa, was no longer amused.

14. The following, referenced excerpts from Russell's published writings have been taken from a 1980 book compiled by a team of writers assigned by me to compile this report; the nominal author who assumed the position of editor for this project was Carol White: *The New Dark Ages Conspiracy* (New York: New Benjamin Franklin Publishing Company, 1980).

15. (London: George Allen and Unwin, 1923).

16. (New York: Simon & Schuster, 1953).

effect on this increase, which continued through each of the world wars.... War ... has hitherto been disappointing in this respect ... but perhaps bacteriological war may prove more effective. If a Black Death could spread throughout the world once in every generation, survivors could procreate freely without making the world too full.... The state of affairs might be somewhat unpleasant, but what of it? Really high-minded people are indifferent to happiness, especially other people's." Russell yearns for a world controlled by a medieval aristocracy, in which "the present urban and industrial centers will have become derelict, and their inhabitants, if still alive, will have reverted to the peasant hardships of their medieval ancestors."

Lord Bertrand Russell was just as nasty as H.G. Wells, and continued the latter's efforts for utopian World Government.

Then, in the same book, he presents his own personal motives, his British oligarchical hatred directed against our United States:

"As for public life, when I first became politically conscious Gladstone and Disraeli still confronted each other amid Victorian solidities, the British Empire seemed eternal, the country was rich, aristocratic, and growing richer.... For an old man, with such a background, it is difficult to feel at home in a world of ... American supremacy."

In reading those quoted passages, you must remind yourself, that the attitude expressed by Russell is not that of some isolated case of a British eccentric; Russell is, as I have emphasized at the outset of this report, a key figure among those who have largely shaped the policies of contemporary post-Nineteenth-Century Liberalism, especially that of the English-speaking world.

The entire Liberal establishment of the United States, when the term "Liberal" is properly employed, is a product of precisely that British Liberalism which the aristocratic Russell not only typifies, but in which he has played a very large part, together with the Fabian Society and his more earthy, plebeian political sibling H.G. Wells. What I have cited from his writings in this location is typical of the kind of thinking we meet today in the public expressions of the Royal Consort, Prince Philip, of World Wildlife Fund (WWF) notoriety, and with Philip's late close associate, Nazi-SS veteran Prince Bernhard, or with the views expressed by Prince Charles and Charles' lackey, and former U.S. Vice-President, Al Gore.

Against such evil fellows as those British types and their American flunkeys, the silly variety of typical U.S. citizen, with his so-called "practical" opinions, is virtually "putty in their hands," is a poor fellow who believes almost any piece of sophist "explanation" by which he is cheating himself of his liberty, and, perhaps, his life, and that of his family, too. The American fool of that type, is his own worst enemy, who does not recognize the Satanic quality of the British imperial crowd which Russell describes with such brutal candor.

To understand the significance of the crisis of the U.S. auto industry, we must clear away the fog of popular delusions which envelop and protect the intention expressed by Britain's Prince Philip and his late accomplice, Nazi-SS veteran Prince Bernhard's role behind the project of the World Wildlife Fund, to continue the intentions of Adolf Hitler's regime by reducing the present world population from a level of about six-and-a-half billions, to about two billions persons.[17]

Ignorant people in high places in Europe or the Americas, believe that simple financial profit and the

______

17. On the occasion of his marriage to the Dutch princess (January, 1937), Bernhard signed his letter of resignation from the Nazi-SS to Hitler personally with a salutary "Heil Hitler!" In those days Nazis were popular with Anglo-Dutch leading circles, including, for a time, Winston Churchill himself. Why not? After all, it had been Hjalmar Schacht's sponsor, Bank of England chief, Brown Brothers, Harriman associate, Montagu Norman who had orchestrated bringing Hitler into power, during times prior to the Nazis' breaking the eastern boundary of France's and the Netherlands' borders.

like, are the glue which holds imperial passions, such as those of the British Empire, together. On the contrary, it is the same aristocratic principle affirmed by Russell, the security of a social system of aristocratic world rule, which is the underlying motive of the feudalist imperial power, not the mere financial gain as such which the Anglo-Dutch Liberal financier interest treasures as the principal economic interest of imperial power. The financier robber-baron of the Anglo-Dutch Liberal stripe, or a similarly corrupted American, desires nothing as passionately as being "born again" as a "Euro-aristocrat."[18] It is those systems, including physical-economic progress, which tend to undermine the power of international monetarist usury, which imperial agents such as Prince Philip are determined to destroy, if they can not prevent them.

The foolish American fails to recognize that the United States has never been menaced by any actually formidable, ultimate enemy, who was not essentially a tool of that British Empire which had set the Japan of 1895-1945 for war against us, and others, and which is setting us up for similar sorts of surrogates' attacks upon us right now.

How and why do you imagine that Prime Minister Tony Blair, through lies and possibly a relevant assassination of one who exposed his fraud, induced the U.S.A. to buy a pack of British lies which brought us, under Dick Cheney's pawn, silly President George W. Bush, Jr., into a long wasting war in Iraq during which we virtually lost our U.S.A. ground forces, while also thoroughly wrecking what had remained of our U.S. economy.[19]

There are numerous bad Americans, but the bad Americans would not have succeeded in ruining us as they have done, but for far too many just-plain-dumb Americans, including some Harvard graduates, especially those of the Baby Boomer class.

Think of the things to which I have just pointed, and you may be on the verge of understanding the current crisis in the cult of American auto-eroticism.

---

18. Imagine a figure such as the notable "Greasy-thumbed Guzik" being "born again" as "Lord Chicago." The late Max Fisher might say, either "Why not?" or "Kill him as one who has become an inconvenient person."

19. Look at the peerage scandals under Blair's ministry. Imagine, the presently unlikely case in which the present Prime Minister is being recreated as "Lord George." Ah, where is our dear Jonathan Swift when we need him? After all, George H.W. Bush was knighted. Is it possible that rancher George W., Jr. might be elevated to the rank of squire?

The Myth of the Automobile

Since the aftermath of the Napoleonic wars, the center of all credible threats to a British empire with Habsburg appendages trailing after, has been the United States of America's role as a bastion of the kind of alternative expressed by the intentional design of our Federal Constitution, its Preamble most notably. It is on exactly this point, that any competent understanding of the causes for the rise and fall of the U.S. auto industry depends, and that absolutely. There can be no competent psychological understanding of the recent crisis of that auto industry, and of the cure of that sickness, from any different standpoint.

There are two principal aspects of that cause of conflict at this present time. First, uppermost, is the British Empire's persuasion that its successful corruption of the U.S.A. culture has brought the U.S. into the pitiable condition at which London's assets, such as the ideologues Felix Rohatyn and London's own leading drug-trade-pusher and foreign agent George Soros could bring down the U.S.A. once and for all, thus clearing the way for the elimination of other obstacles, such as China, India, and Russia. Second, is the orchestration of the social-political-cultural processes inside the U.S.A. which are intended to ruin the U.S.A. to British advantage as from the inside. The auto-industry case is exemplary, for this reason.

Today, there is a cry to save our automobile industry. That is a childish far cry from reality, and I am well-qualified to speak of this, since I have the hash-marks of a leader in the recent economic war to end the insanity which Ford's McNamara and Wall Street control of General Motors caused, my commitment to save the actually useful features of that industry, as I gained those stripes, in February 2006, when the leaders of the Congress and most leaders of the major parties had thrown the entire industry on the dump, all on the orders of swindlers like Felix Rohatyn. What had I said about that issue since the end of 2004 and the very beginning of 2005? Let us consult the record, and ask: who was right, and who did, and is still doing wrong?

Let us also settle accounts with the foolish people who propose to save that industry itself, rather than save the machine-tool capability of which that industry is merely an aspect.

I said, again and again:

I said that we could not save the auto industry on its present scale of operations. Try that, and you not only lose that industry, but you wreck the chances for organizing a recovery of a U.S. economy which is already careening down the highway toward bankruptcy Hell. Some idiots (or, worse) listened to the Felix Rohatyn of Pinochet fame; you can blame them, if you wish, but you should really blame yourself for being either stupid enough, cowardly enough, or crooked enough to believe him. I said, repeatedly, we must save the auto industry by taking it back to its roots, to the development of the machine-tool industry which created the auto industry as one of its many lines of products.

Stop using the silly name used by the usually silly variety of so-called management consultants: "Auto Industry." Say, instead, "That machine-tool sector which enabled us to win World War II, while also rescuing the U.S. economy from the great Depression which Coolidge and Hoover built."

I said then, that we must hive off, for other employment, those sections of what is called the "auto industry," which contain two elements. First, and foremost: the machine-tool design sector as such. Secondly, and that only secondly, the portion of the general manufacturing labor-force which is associated with those relevant elements of the machine-tool sector which must be redirected back to the kind of manifold missions that sector fulfilled during periods such as World Wars I and II. We earmarked specific plants of the so-called auto industry, which should be reclassified to this effect.

In presenting this specific subject-matter, I must also point out the way in which the auto industry was wrecked from the inside, as since the days of that misguided accountant, Robert "Slickum" McNamara, relative to the development of the auto industry in Asia, notably Japan and Korea, and, to a significant degree in pre-1989 Germany. It was the U.S.A.'s playing down the crucial role which must be played by emphasis on scientifically advanced machine-tool design, which set up that U.S. industry for its downfall. In effect, General Motors wrecked the railroads, and then, by the same methods, bankrupted itself.

The first step toward saving that sector of the U.S. economy now, is to get rid of the financier interests which have had full responsibility for wrecking and looting that industry in the first place. Get the paws of Felix Rohatyn and his like out of all strategically important aspects of the U.S. economy.

In 2004-2005, I proposed that the U.S. Federal Government, which has the primary responsibility for that basic economic infrastructure which silly incumbent U.S. governments have been casting adrift since 1967-

A skilled technician works on the Northstar V8 SC engine for General Motors. What's crucial about the auto industry is not that it makes cars, but that it represents a core machine-tool development potential. As shown in World War II, that capability can be used to build virtually anything, from airplanes to nuclear power plants, provided the national leadership exists to make it happen.

68, must, like the legendary Rip Van Winkle, come awake again, to create the categories of infrastructure which we have lost to deliberate ruin, by attrition and intentional neglect over the now nearly forty years of Federal lunacy and the reign of the Baby-Boomer sect of former Vice-President Al Gore, et al.

Large-scale water management, such as the desperately needed rescue of the Mississippi basin which drains the area of the nation between the two principal North-South riparian systems. Get the trucks and private autos largely off the highway to national ruin, by providing a modern rail- or maglev-based transcontinental transport system for the principal modes of transport of passengers and freight. Get out of the rust-bin by launching a national nuclear-power network, the only economically competent system available for today and our future, and instead of relying upon the less efficient, and much more costly imported petroleum for power, use high-energy-flux-density nuclear power systems to generate local and regional supplies of hydrogen-based synthetic fuels for aircraft and automobiles, in addition to producing fuels for regional heating and air conditioning in the principal local and regional areas of habitation. Use these types of large-scale Federal and auxiliary state and local infrastructure projects to generate expanded agriculture and manufacturing, while ending the monstrously silly and wasteful overgrowth of "white collar" employment, by returning to emphasis on actually productive forms of employment, with emphasis on increased rations of employment in categories of all-purpose machine-tool design and experiment.

Under such programs, the ration of automobiles required, per capita, per square kilometer, and per hour of the per-capita day, would be reduced to a sizeable fraction of the current ratio. Hours per day of commuting time would be eliminated, or substantially reduced, giving children their parents back again, and ending the situation in which it is difficult for adults to recall exactly whom they can recall as the identity of their spouse.

Let's get back to being human again.

Therefore, let's divide the form of machine-tool design and related categories between a shrunken auto industry employment, and a greatly expanded variety of alternatives, once again. Let us save the states, cities, and other local communities, and families, we are presently permitting to be destroyed, destroyed through policies of people such as Felix Rohatyn and Britain's anti-American agent, and drug-traffic promoter George Soros. Let us put the full capacity of what some people thought was just an auto industry back into operation again, by putting the emphasis on the principle of science-driven machine-tool design, rather than taking in each other's laundry, if you still have laundry worth washing.

Robert "Slickum" McNamara, with his MBA from Harvard Business School, wrecked the Ford Motor Co. (1946-1962), using accounting methods comparable to the insane "body count" methods he would later use in the Vietnam War, as Secretary of Defense. He is shown here in 1964.

4. The Case of Russia in Eurasia

As we turn our attention now to Eurasia, with emphasis on the role of Eurasian Russia in Asia generally, we must not lose sight of the fact that this chapter's discussion addresses a situation in which the so-called Baby-Boomer generation, with its strategic factor of neoteny, is a leading controlling factor, functionally, of that generation's presently dominant role in several governments, and therefore a crucial factor of the 1968-2008 crisis in the world as a whole. The Baby Boomer factor, the factor of neoteny, is key for understanding the presently manifest sheer lunacy of the current behavior of the U.S. government, the leading U.S. political parties, the special, controlling role of the British government's BAE and related connections to the crucial role of Saudi Arabia, and the sheer lunacy steering the present international monetary-financial situation.

Back during the 1970s, I had a New York City meeting with an Israeli gentleman who was one of the celebrated statesmen of the preceding decades. At one point, he put in a word of caution: Do not forget that some leaders of the region (to which our conversation was devoted) "are clinically insane." He expanded; I could not but agree.

The case of Russia in Eurasia is a phase-spatial aspect of a world situation which, itself, is dominated by the "Baby Boomer" factor in, especially, the Americas and western and central Europe. Such are the dynamics of the present world situation. Worse than insane individual heads of state or government, is the insanity of a dominant layer of several governments, a layer like the neotenous Baby-Boomer element dominating key institutions of a number of crucially important governments today. The recent incident in Georgia should remind us, that this factor of insanity is a factor with which Russia, in particular, is contending today, not only in Georgia.

As a citizen of the U.S.A., I am worrying about the security of a nation which should be a key, cooperating partner of the U.S.A., Russia. Russia's economic security is therefore an important part of U.S. strategic self- interests. My worry is not just about Russians. It is my worry about the important physical-economic role which Russia must play in the present and future economy of the world at large, and, also, how the lack of progress in this area affects the U.S.A. I am worry-

Courtesy of Dr. Sergei Cherkasov and Academician Dmitri Rundqvist

An oil-drilling site in Siberia. Russia's disproportionate reliance on its natural resources is a problem that should concern us all.

ing about a lack of truly modern Russian successes in the area of non-military production there, and, therefore, my worry about Russia's tendency toward disproportionate economic reliance on what are otherwise, admittedly, its treasures of natural resources.

This is a Russian problem; but, the effect which should concern us the most, is the fact that the problem involved is essentially global. This is the case, since Russia is the keystone of the entire Eurasian continental system of economic development, and its agricultural and machine-tool grade manufacturing capabilities ought to be recognized as a much-needed, contributing factor for the survival of the world economy as a whole.

The crucial conceptual problem which I am addressing at this point in this report, is a prevalent failure in theoretical economics, one which is generic for the prevalent systems of accounting and physical economy, in nearly all cases, world-wide today. For example: no nation appears to have become capable, so far, of understanding the true meaning of "profit." In fact, because of the influence of monetarist forces in financial accounting over thinking about today's economic theory, and related governmental programs, today's taught economics is intrinsically incompetent in respect to the tasks posed by the physical results needed, per capita and per square kilometer of the territory of na-

tions.

The other name for that problem is: a lack of mastery of true, individual, human creativity.

The world we have entered since the financial crises of 1997-98, is a different world than existed earlier. Although the trend in the world economy since 1968-73 was, indeed, already insane, the continuing decay in both leading institutions and in the shift of power in government and corporate life, toward the Baby-Boomer generation, has introduced a growing factor of sheer insanity into the world system, such that the already bad systems of the late 1960s and early 1970s, were shifted into a condition of sheer insanity under the changes in international economy under the impact of the role of the Trilateral Commission's violently destructive influence on the international monetary-financial and economic-social systems. What had been the onset of cancer in the body of the patient, has become the patient.

Thus, the problem now is, that the concept of true scientific and related creativity as such, is not a concept included, even in a peripheral way, in the language of the practiced economic doctrines of nations, or economists generally, today. On close scrutiny, in the leading economic circles of most nations, today, the term "economic science" usually means, ordinary, green-eye-

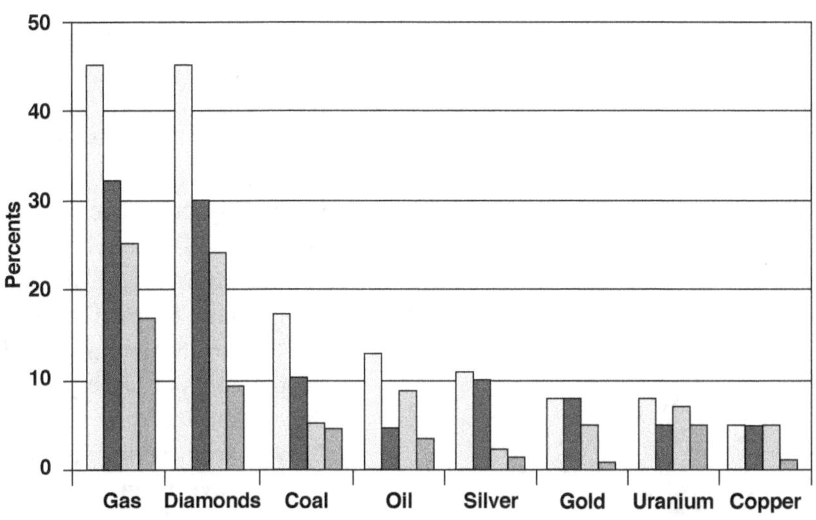

TABLE 1

Russia's Share of World Resource and Reserves vs. Production and Consumption

Courtesy of Dr. Sergei Cherkasov and Academician Dmitri Rundqvist

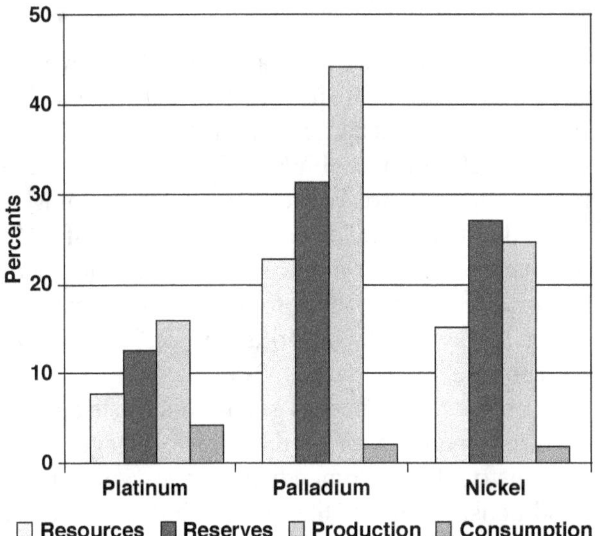

FIGURE 2

Russia's Share of Platinum Group Metals, Resources and Reserves, vs. Production and Consumption

Courtesy of Dr. Sergei Cherkasov and Academician Dmitri Rundqvist

shade traditions of ordinary financial accounting, or simply a consulting charlatan's sales-pitch, dressed up, for the edification of the credulous, as if with some silly frills integrated into an ill-fitting clown suit. Under presently deteriorating conditions, even traditional ac-counting practice itself becomes, clinically, insanity.

The magic word which best identifies what the experts of most nations have lacked, even before the developments of late 1960s and 1970s, is, so to speak, "creativity." "Creativity," which is the crucial issue of this report on required economic measures, is properly defined, descriptively, as the essential, absolute difference between man and beast. The problem which I am emphasizing here, is one whose origins have arisen from that kind of lack of creativity. Even among leaders of nations, and many scientists as well, there was already a lack of knowledge of that which has been denied by what that great Classical tragedian Aeschylus portrayed as the evil Olympian Zeus of Aeschylus' drama ***Prometheus Bound.***

For as long as a significant factor of actual physical productivity gains was influential within the worsening crisis situation of the late 1960s, as long as the manned Moon landing was still a theme in popular opinion, there was an element of sanity in policy-making, an element of sanity which vanished over the interval of the U.S. Carter Administration. With the rise of "environmentalism" and "globalization," the factor of traditional sanity seemed to go down the drain. However, the corrupting factor was, in principle, an ancient one, as Classical Greek tragedy should remind us.

In ***Prometheus Bound***, Aeschylus had portrayed that Olympian tyrant Zeus as torturing Prometheus for the alleged "crime" of imparting knowledge of the use of "fire" to mortal men and women. In real history, most societies have been ruled by agencies, which, like the Olympian Zeus of that drama, forbade the individual members of the mass of the subject population from discovering those principles of nature which fit that drama's category of "fire."

What is called "globalization" is a swindle intended for a kindred sort of anti-humanistic effect. In that case, the avowed intention of the British and other ideologues involved today, is that every nation should depend upon the production by other nations for even its food supplies and other subsistence. This is the design for a global form of a "Tower of Babble," in which financial

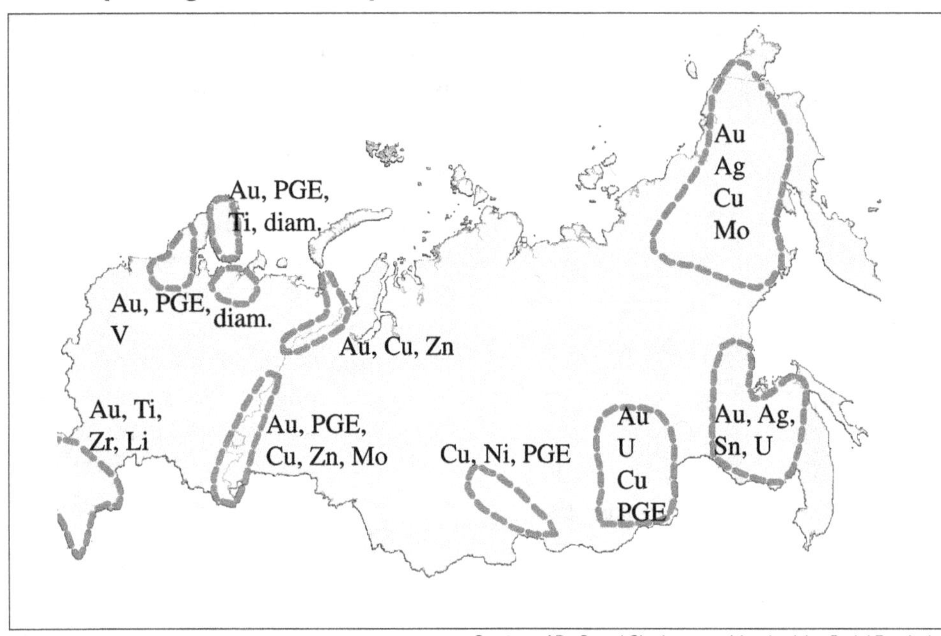

Courtesy of Dr. Sergei Cherkasov and Academician Dmitri Rundqvist

speculators sit between and prey upon the flow of goods from farmer to eater, paying the least amount, and extracting the highest price at the consumer-end of the flow.

For most of the societies, and their cultures of which we have actual knowledge, including most European nations and the U.S.A. today, not only are the so-called lower economic strata condemned to this suppression of their human creative potential. Even the most powerful ruling circles, while better informed in some respects, have no actual knowledge of those kinds of principles of creativity which the Olympian Zeus demanded be hidden.

Since the problem of creativity is essentially a matter of social relations, social processes, the best insight into this problem is usually found not among physical scientists today, but in the great Classical tragedies of ancient Greece and the modern dramas of Shakespeare and Friedrich Schiller. Like the mortal men and women of Homer's *Iliad*, or the great Classical Greek tragedies, the mortal members of society, usually extended from the highest political ranks to the lowest social grades, are victims of what are for them "invisible forces," forces corresponding to the imaginary evil gods who dominate the mortals of the *Iliad*, or

the echoes of the same view of tragedy by the Classical Greek tragedians, or by the characters of each of the tragedies of Shakespeare.

Contrary to modern English-speaking and kindred Romantics, the true principle of Classical tragedy is that it is virtually the entire society which is self-doomed by the controlling role of mental habits and adopted beliefs which prevent virtually all of the members of society, as in the Schiller-Verdi *Don Carlos*, from acting in what should have been the obvious way of freeing oneself and one's society from the grip of those customs and related beliefs of the society virtually as a whole, which would cause the society as a whole to virtually destroy itself, rather than offend one of those accustomed beliefs.[20]

So, the tragedy of European civilization, over the interval from the 1890 discharge of Chancellor Otto von Bismarck, a discharge done in the interest of the Kaiser's uncle, Prince of Wales Edward Albert, condemned Europe to two World Wars, to the rise of Mussolini and Hitler, to the so-called "Cold War" of 1945-1989, and the threat of a new such "world war" today. The typically tragic modern fool of today, responds to that fact, by saying, "What British empire? I don't see a British empire."

It was not ignorance as such which caused such tragedies, in real life, or on the Classical stage. It was the Sophistry of accustomed belief, or so-called "popular traditions," of belief like that of the mortals of the *Iliad* or later Greek tragedies, in the existence and the will of the "gods."

This practice of "traditionalist" suppression of the creative mental potentials of the majority of the subject population, has been the characteristic of the known imperial systems of western Asia, and their European

____

20. Schiller-Verdi: "Beware the Grand Inquisitor!"

successors, since the evil Delphi cult of Gaea-Python, or Apollo-Dionysus. This was the Roman Empire, Byzantium, the Venetian-Norman system of the Crusaders and their Venetian loan-shark financiers, and of the efforts to revive such imperial systems, such as the Anglo-Dutch Liberal finance-imperial system of modern times.

Thus, society imprisons and repeatedly destroys itself for the sake of obedience to the implicitly perceived pleasure of the pagan household gods of each relevant culture's version of a Pantheon.

In the Liberal form of imperialism, which was crafted by Paolo Sarpi in the form of northern European culture known as Anglo-Dutch imperial Liberalism, the same suppression of the human knowledge of the actually creative powers specific to the individual human mind, has appeared in a relatively new guise. The phrase, "magic of the marketplace," is typical of the modern Sophist's suppression of knowledge of the role of human individual creativity in generating that physical and cultural innovation on which all increases of the productive powers of labor depend, per capita and per square kilometer of territory.

To Free Humanity

To secure those urgent goals urgently required for today, we must uproot all vestiges of the inherently tragic, recent drive toward "globalization," not only to return to emphasis on the role of the perfectly sovereign nation-state *and its culture*, but also to do this from the standpoint already expressed by the principle of the 1648 Peace of Westphalia. In other words, a system of respectively sovereign nation-states bound together by *the common principle of the benefit of the other*.

This confronts us with four leading, shared challenges for the planet as a whole.

1.) Raising the price of labor to the levels of national productivity at which prices are not driven so low "competitively," that some nations, largely representing the great majority of humanity, can not afford to employ the lower eighty percentile of their populations, by commitment to developing modern standards for standard of life and employment of the entire national population. This means high rates, per capita and per square kilometer of scientific and technological progress embodied within the body of production. This is achieved through investing the marginal increase in protected price, in increasing the productivity of all parts of the population, including what are presently the poorest.

2.) Developing the raw materials of the planet to such effect that all nations will be assured reasonable access to the purpose of providing the raw materials required for the uplifting of the preponderance of their population as a whole.

3.) The rates of development of raw materials, throughout the planet as a whole, must be advanced for the benefit of the population of the nations as a whole.

4.) The rates of scientific progress needed to realize those objectives must be supported.

The territory of Russia and adjoining nations of Eurasia and its nearby waters, embodies a crucial part of both the development of raw materials and scientific progress needed by neighboring nations of Asia. The crucial thing is not access to the land-area in which such resources lie, but the quality of fundamental scientific progress needed to gather such resources and process them in ways suited for the needs of both Russia and its neighbors.

Therefore, in the case of Russia itself, it is the underdevelopment of Russia's previously established, relatively unique scientific potential in large categories of science and technology, which calls our attention to the terribly destructive, and vicious effects of the looting of the territory and scientific institutions of the former Soviet Union during the greater part of the decade of the 1990s.

Therefore, the limitation of economic goals to proportionately excessive emphasis on harvesting of so-called "natural resources," is a hazardous enterprise in the end. I explain here, echoing what I have stated in my recently published ***Russia's Role in a Recovery***.[21] Russia's management of raw materials from an advanced scientific standpoint, is clearly of crucial importance for both Russia and its neighbors. The present danger, is that, presently, the dependency on a flow of income from export of raw materials, becomes an extremely problematic course over a period of the medium term. The balance must be adjusted, to put advanced productive goals for scientific progress in production, and ex-

____

21. See *EIR*, Sept. 5, 2008.

FIGURE 4

Planned Russian Railroad Development of 2030

To reverse the 1990s looting of Russia, and the ongoing excessive emphasis on harvesting so-called "natural resources," requires expansion of scientific progress in production, including the development of infrastructure. This EIR *map of projected rail construction is based on a Russian Railways map titled "Prospective Topology of the Russian Federation's Rail Network Development until 2030." Among the "railroads of strategic importance," planned for construction between 2015 and 2030, is the line from the Lena River near Yakutsk to the Bering Strait at Uelen. From there, in cooperation with the United States, a rail-tunnel should be built across the Strait, to Alaska.*

pansion of the productive base, to a higher place on the agenda, not merely for economic reasons, but for the continued overall cultural viability of Russia itself.

As I expressed this on public occasions such as my notable Berlin Kempinski Hotel address of October 12, 1988, it was clear to me, then, as a U.S. figure engaged in relevant policy discussions of prospects for future cooperation between the Soviet Union and both the U.S.A. and Europe. This option existed, but only in the case that the U.S.A., Britain, and France's President Mitterrand, had not adopted their savage ruin and looting of the former Soviet Union, and of Germany and the former Comecon states, a looting which was effected through what became the Maastricht doctrine and adjunct measures targeting continental Europe, including Russia. This looting was greatly aided through the British use of its foreign agent George Soros, to wreck the European Rate Mechanism. Conse-

EIRNS/Rachel Douglas

"We who are civilized," LaRouche writes, "must assume the moral and intellectual leadership in treating what should be considered by coming generations as the common aims of mankind." Shown, LaRouche (right) in Moscow in 1994, with the late Pobisk G. Kuznetsov, a leader of the Russian scientific community. LaRouche addressed Kuznetsov's "President" group, at the Academy of Sciences.

quently, the per capita condition of life in relevant parts of the Eurasian continent would have been progressive, as opposed to the vast, mass-murderous orgy of economic rape targeting Germany as also the former Comecon nations, a looting which has been fostered through Soros' accomplices during that decade, and longer.

My forecasts of the trend leading into 1989 had been on the books of nations, so to speak, since 1983,[22] when I forecast the danger of a Soviet economic collapse "in about five years" if certain measures were not taken in the meantime. The crash against which I warned took six years, not five, but no one otherwise known publicly, had any idea that such a development could occur. Even when I had forecast, in October 1988, an early 1989 Polish crisis leading to the threatened collapse of the Comecon, and then Russia, later, the U.S. Adminis-

tration of my personal adversary President George H.W. Bush, showed no inkling of the reality that such developments were already afoot.

As a result of the combination of ignorance and ham-handed follies, by both the U.S.A. and western and central Europe from 1989 on, those nations are now bankrupt, looted paupers compared to their condition then.

From the standpoint of the informed knowledge of competent U.S. circles, economic partnership, on an equitable basis, between the U.S.A. and Russia today, is an indispensable precondition for not only the welfare of those two nations, but, in fact, the world as a whole.

Take into account, but also prepare to put aside, the lunacies which are admittedly rampant in certain circles within the U.S.A. today; we must cooperate between Russia and the U.S., as with other parts of this planet, on the basis of an up-to-date version of the great principle of the Peace of Westphalia. As our great Benjamin Franklin once said of the relations among those North American colonies menaced by the evil British Empire, so the representatives of the U.S.A. and Russia should speak today: "We must, indeed, all

---

22. That forecast was first delivered, by me, confidentially, in late February 1983, in my discussions with the Soviet representative involved in those exploratory U.S.-Soviet discussions. Later, after things turned nasty in the late Spring, I repeated the forecast publicly, but without referring publicly to the February discussion itself. At that point in the game, I was still bound not to reveal what might be classified materials.

hang together or, most assuredly, we shall all hang separately."

Thus, to illustrate the larger scope of the principle involved, the common interest of the U.S.A., Russia, China, and India, typifies the principle which we must deploy in concert for the purpose of bringing together the sovereign nation-states of this planet as a whole.

That said, as a matter of explanation, most among those in the U.S.A. who may be considered well-informed, do not see a needed present balance among raw materials development, agriculture, manufacturing, science, and basic economic infrastructure in the current direction of Russia's policy. This is not a matter of a proposed U.S. demand upon Russia, but a well-founded concern for the well-being of Russia as an important partner. We have a mutual interest in Russia's success in these matters, and should discuss the matter accordingly. Forget the British and their ideological partners for the moment; we who are civilized must assume the moral and intellectual leadership in treating what should be considered by coming generations as the common aims of mankind.

The Present Crisis In Economics

In the closing sentence of his celebrated 1854 habilitation dissertation, Professor Bernhard Riemann ends the dissertation with a sentence in which he warns that the treatment of the problems of mathematics which he has just identified in the preceding part of the dissertation as a whole, must be transferred from the department of mathematics, to that of physics. Only a minority of scientists since, such as the opponents of modern positivism and of Bertrand Russell's numerology, opponents of positivism and numerology such as Max Planck and Albert Einstein, have understood the fuller significance of that closing sentence of the *Habilitationsschrift*. Students of Aeschylus' *Prometheus Bound* should understand my point.

Instead, we have been belabored, in university classrooms and elsewhere, with both the dogma of Paolo Sarpi and such of his ideological descendants of the empiricist school, such as Abraham de Moivre, D'Alembert, Leonhard Euler, Lagrange, Laplace, Cauchy, et al., in their silly and arbitrary notion of the so-called "imaginary." As a result of the influence of such reductionists as the modern empiricists, positivists, or the radical school of Bertrand Russell's devotees, or the kindred descendants of the ancient Sophists, the idea of a universal principle and its formal expres-

sion in mathematical forms, has been lost from most classrooms, despite the precise warning by Albert Einstein, lost to most of even those ranked as scientists.

The practical issue of economy here, is a matter of the actual, ontological implications of the notion of a universal physical principle, as Einstein emphasized this in defining the physical universe as finite, but without external boundaries. These ideas, from the ancient Classical Greeks, as given rebirth by Nicholas of Cusa and his followers, are, as Einstein emphasized, pivoted in the modern classroom on the subject of the uniquely original discovery of the principle of universal gravitation by Kepler, in which the relationship of the universal physical principles which define the universe as experimentally finite, is coupled with the ontologically infinitesimal expression of that principle in experimental practice.

This relationship, as Einstein recognized the present-day authority of Kepler's discovery, is reflected in individual human experience as the notion of *creativity*. The discovery of such a principle, which takes the experience out of the more limited domain of earlier experimental knowledge, typifies the quality of the human mind which corresponds, ontologically, to the notion of that human creativity which distinguishes the human individual's mental potentials from the behavioral limitations of the lower forms of life.

The problem which tends to prevent even students trained in physical science from grasping the notion of the experimentally demonstrated existence of anti-entropic creativity, is indoctrination in the reductionist method in the history of mathematics since the aprioristic, Aristotelean hoax of **Euclid's Elements**, or comparable intellectual impedimenta.

Creativity is, ontologically, the valid experimental demonstration of the existence of an efficient, "commandable" principle which lies outside the domain of what was previously considered the self-boundaries of reality. Unfortunately, the modern classroom, including the modern university classroom, is often as dumb as rocks in this matter.

To illustrate that point in a manner relevant to the issues of economy and society treated here, permit me the following, admittedly cute illustration of the point.

Captain Nudnik Beams Down

If you were, for example, a Captain Nudnik from Vega first encountering the human species on Earth, how would you know the difference between, on the

Artist's conception of the Magnetrain. The Magnetrain is one proposed design for a magnetic levitation system for high-speed rail, which promises an efficient passenger and freight-handling system to develop the world, link continents, and solve urban traffic congestion.

one side, men and women, and, on the other side, the beasts? Suppose you, playing the role of that Captain Nudnik, were assigned to breed an intelligent species selected from among the fauna of Earth. Since Nudnik would not speak the local language, how would he know which was which?

He might wish to rely on a notion which is typical of the circles with which Julian Huxley was associated professionally: *potential relative population-density.* Now consider, *the three more obvious of the degrees of freedom which express the essential, absolute distinction of man from beast.*

In animal ecology, there is a balance among the species inhabiting a given territory, such that for each species-variety, there is a definable phase-space of each species (relative to the others) which represents a variable relative boundary condition within which the variable population-potential is fixed (as for example, between foxes and the prey called rabbits). With mankind, this kind of limiting function does not exist; a different kind of boundary-function is pertinent.

For man, there is first, the variability of the function of simple per-capita values, relative to the environment. Man's expressed power to innovate technologically, changes that function in a way not existing among lower forms of life. On a second level, man is able to offset the depletion of a specific, previously required element of the environment by discoveries of principle in human technique. On a third level, man creates artificial entire environments, even to the extent of creating new elements to become determining features of the society's new environment.

The human mind, by means of a creative faculty which does not exist in the lower forms of life, is able to change its behavior in a fashion associated with the discovery of universal physical principles, principles which transform the mentality of human beings to the same effect we would otherwise expect only in the evolution of a qualitatively higher form of new species.

This specific power of the human mind is unique among all known living species. The included effect of this cognitive evolution, upward, of the human mind, evolution as expressed through science and Classical modes of artistic composition, is the origin of the qualitative increase of the potential relative population-density of the human species.

This evolutionary development through human creativity, has two general, categorical types. Physical science and only Classical modes of artistic composition. The faculty of mind in both cases is the same; the difference is the application. In the one case, the human mind is transforming society's action on nature; in the other, it is the social process of transmission of ideas, which is the medium and mode of creativity.

As to the physical-productive side of this matter, the increase of productivity, through innovations at the point of production, is more readily acknowledged. However, the most significant effects occur in the domain of general, basic economic infrastructure, such as the effect of the shift from Solar power, to the higher level of chemical combustion, to the vastly more efficient (per ton of fuel consumed) use of nuclear-fission power, and the use of more physically efficient modes of transport than automobiles, such as rail or maglev. The greatest part of the gains in productivity are found in the impact of advances in basic economic infrastructure upon physical production, and in the promotion of the development of the powers of insight of the human mind achieved, almost exclusively, through scientific or Classical artistic practices.

It is up to the economist to become as intelligent on this subject-matter of the effect of human creativity on increasing the potential relative population-density of mankind as the legendary, very observant Captain Nudnik.

After all, being stranded on Earth, and, therefore, having nothing much to do otherwise, a poor Nudnik had no choice of occupation so well-suited to his circumstances as studying, and promoting human creative behavior.

The Machine-Tool Principle

The most significant economic activity in production is the production of the means of production themselves. Thus, to limit the latter, as what might be assumed to be an economic measure, for the sake of building automobiles, for example, is utter physical-economic incompetence. Thus, it was the spin-offs from the Kennedy Moon-Landing program, which contributed the relatively highest rate of physical return on investment of virtually all production in the U.S.A. during the relevant period.

Thus, it was failing to put the machine-tool sector associated with the auto industry first and foremost, above the auto industry itself, which was the great idiocy in the economic policy which located the greatest economic benefit of production to be in the cars, rather than the higher technology of the machine-tool sector itself, and the creation of relevant forms of basic economic infrastructure. It is not infrastructure as such which provides this benefit, but the *toll-free public infrastructure* which increases the net productive powers of labor per capita and per square kilometer, for the society as a whole, that at a greater rate than at any point of production investment.

Similarly, it is the employment of Classical artists, physical scientists, and an advancing quality of universal health-care system and pensions, the human aspects of basic economic infrastructure in general, which must enjoy, together with science and the machine-tool sector, the relatively greatest degree of preference in the expenditure and investment by society in all sectors.

The way to higher productivity is not the immediate output of some people, but the development of the general environment defined by the society as a whole, the society within whose development the great catalyst of increased productivity is concentrated.

www.ingramcontent.com/pod-product-compliance
Lightning Source LLC
Chambersburg PA
CBHW080239260726
48658CB00008B/3168